THE REFINER'S FIRE

MARVIN MOORE

Pacific Press Publishing Association
Boise, Idaho
Oshawa, Ontario, Canada

Edited by Glen Robinson
Designed by Linda Griffith
Cover by Eric Meola/Image Bank ©
Type set in 10/12 Century Schoolbook

The author assumes full responsibility for the accuracy of
facts and quotations cited in this book.

Unless otherwise indicated, Scripture references in this book
are from the New International Version.

Library of Congress Catalog Card Number: 88-84130

ISBN 0-8163-0829-2

90 91 92 93 94 • 5 4 3 2 1

Foreword

For more than 100 years, Revelation 14:6-12 has inspired Seventh-day Adventists to warn the world of the momentous issues that lie ahead. We believe God has commissioned us, more than any other Christian body, to prepare men and women for the close of probation and the second coming of Christ. One of my greatest desires is to see North American Adventists appreciate this privilege and accept this sacred responsibility with all their heart and soul.

In *The Refiner's Fire*, Marvin Moore reviews the evidence that tells us who we are and why God has placed us in the world at this time. He also challenges us to accept God's plan as a personal mandate in this final hour of earth's history. Unfortunately, extreme positions regarding the preparation needed for the end time have caused a great deal of conflict in our church, particularly during the latter half of the twentieth century. On the other hand, it must be recognized that any discussion of God's plan for His church today compels us to take these issues into account. Marvin has tried to clarify the issues rather than debate them. I encourage each reader to approach what he says in the same spirit.

I urge you to share this book with your friends. Wherever possible, meet together to discuss these things in small groups, praying that the Holy Spirit will lead you to understand His plan for you. Encourage your pastor to conduct a prayer meeting series, using this book and similar material as a basis for study.

It is my earnest hope that this book will help many Seventh-day Adventists gain a new and enlarged vision of God's design for their lives.

Neal C. Wilson, President
General Conference of SDA

Contents

Preface

Before you begin reading, I would like to say a few words about the kind of book this is—and the kind it is not. This is not a scholarly work. I make no claim to providing you with the results of original research, nor even to analyzing the existing data in ways that Adventists have never thought of before.

Above all else, what you will read in this book is a statement of faith—my faith, and, I believe, that of many of my fellow Adventists. I hope it will become the faith of many Adventists who have not understood their history and mission in quite the light that I present them.

Often a tension exists between scholarship and faith. I do not consider this either good or bad, but simply a result of the two approaches to what we know and seek to know. The scholar is trained, and rightly so, to analyze every scrap of data before drawing conclusions, and then to state them with great caution. This scholarly approach to history and the study of God's Word helps keep faith realistic.

Faith, on the other hand, is bold—almost reckless at times.

Faith knows, but overlooks. The author of Hebrews made a statement of faith when he said, "By faith Noah . . . prepared an ark"; "by faith Abraham . . . went out"; "by faith Moses . . . refused to be called the son of Pharaoh's daughter."

Imagine, if you will, the author of Hebrews saying, "By faith Abraham, when he was called to go out, . . . obeyed—though he stayed in Haran till his father died, and when he finally got to Canaan, he let a famine scare him into Egypt, where he lied about his relationship to Sarah."

At times, such insights into Abraham's life are useful—or why would the Bible provide them? It is good for scholars to dig into the past and let it tell us whatever it will, good or bad, about the lives of those in our own movement whom we have come to revere. These discoveries need not weaken our faith that God led our pioneers any more than our knowledge of Abraham's weaknesses and sins weakens faith in God's leading in his life.

But when the author of Hebrews set out to write a positive faith statement about Israel's pioneers, he left all these qualifiers out. He challenged his readers to look at the broad sweep of the patriarchs' lives, not at the unfortunate details. For it was in the broad sweep, and not necessarily in every unfortunate detail, that God's leading in their lives is evident.

Our Adventist history is also checkered with the weaknesses and mistakes of our pioneers. Too often we, like Israel in the wilderness, have grumbled and complained and allowed our humanness to enter into the work God gave us to do. This can be a dangerous field for study, because it is all too easy to let these failures blind us to God's purpose for us and its fulfillment in our history. Yet dangerous or not, it is also important that we understand these things, and our scholars are the best equipped to lead us into a careful investigation of them.

But in spite of our weaknesses and failures, and at times our downright sinfulness, it is still true—with us as it was with Abraham—that God has given us a work to do. Our pioneers took hold of that work to the best of their ability, and it is still God's purpose that we should do the same.

This book is my personal expression of faith in the Adventist movement, offered in full recognition of our checkered past, yet uncluttered by it. In writing it I am particularly indebted to two people: Leroy Froom and Ellen White. Froom's influence is particularly evident in chapters 2 through 4. It would have been impossible for me to write chapter 2 without the aid of his four-volume set, *The Prophetic Faith of Our Fathers*. In a sense, chapter 2 is a distillation of Froom's volumes 1 to 3, and chapter 3 is a distillation of volume 4.

Froom the scholar was also a dedicated Seventh-day Adventist and can perhaps be forgiven, at least by those of us who share his faith, for allowing his faith to intrude into his scholarship. I am sure that his dedication to our movement influenced my views significantly.

In chapters 2 and 4, I have depended heavily on Froom as a source for historical information. Endnotes to these quotations give the original source as listed by Froom in his footnotes, followed by the volume and page number in Froom where the quote may be found. A typical endnote would thus look like this: 1. John Calvin, *Institutes*, 7, vol. 2, p. 314 (Froom, II:437). The Roman numeral in the parentheses represents the volume number and the Arabic numerals the page number in Froom's works. Where I quote Froom himself, the footnote follows the same style.

Adventists and non-Adventists alike recognize that Ellen White made a monumental contribution to the success of our movement. We simply would not be what we are or where we are today without her influence. The many careful investigations into her life and ministry during the last quarter of a century have caused all thinking Adventists to do a great deal of soul-searching. Some lost their faith as a result, but most of us came through that experience with changed assumptions and a renewed commitment to her divine call.

I am aware of the controversies that have surrounded Ellen White's life and work these past few years, and I do not wish to brush aside all the questions that have been raised as insignificant or without validity. But again, I do not believe that in making a clear statement of faith and a call for others to join me in that faith, it is useful to dig up all the problems of the past. There is a time and a place to discuss those things. Many of us have done that and will continue to do so. But that time and place is not now and not here.

A number of people have contributed to the preparation of this book. I would especially like to thank Elder Neal Wilson, the president of our General Conference, for his willingness to read the manuscript and write the Foreword.

I would also like to give special thanks to those who have read the manuscript and shared with you their reactions to it on the back cover: Dr. Herbert Douglass, Dr. Jerry Gladson, and Dr. John Brunt. In addition, Dr. Colin Standish has offered constructive criticism that has significantly enhanced the value of the finished book.

Others who read the manuscript and volunteered their suggestions were Elder Don Mansell, one of my fellow editors at Pacific Press; Elder Don Driver, the pastor of the church I attend in Boise, Idaho; and several members of the Boise church, including attorney Jim Balkins, Bee Biggs, and Steve and Linda Manning.

Last, but certainly not least, I must give credit to my dear wife, Lois, who shares with me so intimately and deeply the aspirations expressed in this book. She never complained about the many hours of time spent in writing, and she willingly endured additional hours of listening as I read page after page of manuscript to her. I used to smile at authors who gave credit to family members for their patience while they wrote. Now I know why they did!

Finally, I would like to give credit to you, my readers, who are willing to devote the many hours of your time that it will take to read this book. I hope your time is rewarded, both with growth in your personal spiritual experience and in your dedication to the cause which we as Adventists have traditionally held so dear.

Marvin Moore
Boise, Idaho
October 16, 1988

One

Who Are We and Why Are We Here?

When I was a kid, I used to enjoy building towers with blocks. As I added block after block, the top of the tower would begin to tremble. With each new block it would sway a little more. Soon I had to be very careful as I added blocks, because the slightest touch would dump the whole thing over. Finally, even with the greatest of care, my tower would crash to the floor.

Some people think the Adventist Church, like that tower, is about to crash to the ground. I doubt it. Our church has withstood worse stresses than those presently confronting us, and we have survived. However, we would be naive to suppose that no trembling is happening at the top. By top I do not mean the administrative leadership in Washington, D.C., but rather the highest spiritual levels of the church—the spiritual leadership in our local churches and conferences, the level of spirituality in our individual lives.

Perhaps a tower of blocks that comes crashing to the floor is the wrong analogy. A better illustration might be a cube of butter set upright on the counter in a warm kitchen. At first, the butter stands firm and tall. Soon, however, the sides begin to soften. The bottom starts to spread, and, in time, everything has settled into an oily puddle on the counter.

Throughout our history, we have believed that Bible prophecy foretold an end-time movement of God's people who would prepare the world for the second coming of Jesus, and who would themselves stand through earth's final crisis to see Him come. We have believed that God raised up our church, the Seventh-day Adventist Church, to be that end-time people. Even a casual glance at Adventist history reveals that we *have* carried our message to nearly every inhabited part of the globe. No other Christian organization—certainly none our size has developed such a worldwide work.

Their vision that we are God's people for this hour drove our pioneers to evangelize the world.

My concern is that the Adventist Church today, especially in North America, is in danger of losing that spiritual vision. Fewer of us today understand who we are, where we came from, and where we are going—or ought to be going. In some cases this shift is deliberate. Some understand very well where we came from and where our pioneers thought we were going, but to their minds the vision of the pioneers was flawed. They want to change the church's course—head it in a different direction.

However, those who feel this way are in the minority. The majority of Adventists today are simply ignorant of our origin, mission, and destiny. October 22, 1844, is a day they remember hearing about. Jesus is coming soon, maybe, and they'll be glad to see Him when He arrives. But in the meantime, there's a job to go to every day, kids to raise, and, if they're lucky, a vacation now and then to enjoy. The affairs of everyday life have become our highest priority. It no longer matters where we came from, why we are here, or where we are going—not because we've given up the vision. Too many of us never knew!

Test my theory for yourself. Next time you're in an Adventist group—a Sabbath School class, perhaps, or a group gathered around a table at a church potluck—ask different ones to tell you what is special about being an Adventist. What's different about us that's also very important? I'm sure there are exceptions, but as a general rule, I suspect you'll find a good bit of confusion and not many clear answers.

That's the trembling at the top, the melting down at the bottom, that concerns me.

I grew up in the Adventist Church, the son of missionaries to South America. Most of my education has been in Adventist schools. I spent fifteen years as a pastor for the church. I can scarcely remember when the mission of our church has not been an important part of my life. Thus it is with sadness that I see the misunderstanding and ignorance of our church's mission among so many of our people today. And it is with the hope that I can dispel some of the ignorance and relieve some of the misunderstanding that I write this book.

So what can you expect to read in the next 200 pages or so?

What this book is about

While I accept the Adventist self-understanding, I am going to assume that many of my Adventist readers are only vaguely familiar with our roots and would like me to say more than just, "This is who we are and what we ought to be doing. Believe it and get busy."

The title of the book, *The Refiner's Fire*, comes from Malachi 3:2-4:

Who can endure the day of his coming? Who can stand when he appears? For he will be like a refiner's fire or a launderer's soap. He will sit as a refiner and purifier of silver; he will purify the Levites and refine them like gold and silver. Then the Lord will have men who will bring offerings in righteousness, and the offerings of Judah and Jerusalem will be acceptable to the Lord, as in days gone by, as in former years.

Ellen White applies this passage to the work that God wants to accomplish in the lives of His people at the present time, and she has explained in some detail what that work encompasses. Some of the things she says seem hard to understand, and some things have been and still are misunderstood. Unfortunately, these misunderstandings have led to a great fear of the end times—perhaps in some instances causing people to actually give up their faith. I recall hearing one girl, for instance, who said, "If only one in twenty will be saved, I might as well give up, because I'm not good enough."

Hence the subtitle of this book: "A message of hope for Adventists awaiting the end time." Adventists need hope—assurance—not only that they can endure the fierce physical hardships of the time of trouble, but more important, that they can be spiritually prepared for that time. Preparation for the end time is not nearly the frightening impossibility that many of us think it is. *God is on our side.* Jesus, our Mediator, is doing everything possible in the heavenly sanctuary to help us make it through. God will not abandon a single one of us at the last minute just because we aren't quite "good enough." Away with such terrible thoughts!

In the first section of this book, "The Great Advent Movement," I will share with you the historical evidence that tells me who we are and why we are here. In the second section, "Preparing for the End Time," I will discuss the misunderstandings that have arisen over the preparation God wants us to make as we look forward to earth's final crisis, and I will explain what I understand that preparation to be and how we can make it. You will see that there is no need to fear.

As we all know, Christ has delayed His coming nearly 150 years since 1844. In the third section, "Living in the End Time," I will say a few words about what I think God wants us to be doing in these closing hours of the delay, just before the final crisis breaks upon us. If what I say makes sense to you, I hope you will join me and many others in doing it. I don't believe we have much time left to complete the task.

A search for reality

Life is a search for reality—for an explanation of our own experience and of the world around us that best matches "what really is." Several hundred years ago, in Western culture, all explanations of "the way things really are" revolved around religion and the church. That is no longer true. Today, nonreligious explanations of "the way things really are" have taken precedence over religious explanations in the public mind. The scientist, in particular, is convinced that his view of reality is closest to what really is, because it is based on what human beings actually observe.

However, religious explanations of reality still abound, and there is still a great deal of faith in Christian explanations of reality that would not make sense to a secular-minded scientist. For example, evangelical and fundamentalist Christians affirm without hesitation that Jesus Christ was born of a virgin, that He died for the sins of mankind, that He rose on the third day from the grave, and that He is alive in heaven today as the Mediator between the human race and God.

Our view of "the way things really are" gives meaning and direction to our lives, often with a passion. Perhaps the best example of this in our modern world is the fundamentalist, fanatical Islamic republic that has been established in Iran. These people are absolutely convinced that their Mohammedan interpretation of reality is correct and that the whole world would be a better place to live if everyone were a Moslem whose devotion and lifestyle matched their own. Their mission, as they see it, is to make the world that way. Anything that stands in the way of that objective is considered a demonic force. Since the United States is the greatest secular power in today's world that stands between them and their objective of worldwide conversion to Islam, America is "the great Satan."

Odd as it may seem, these people are, in some ways, not a great deal different from Seventh-day Adventists. We, too, have a particular view of what the world and life are "really like," and our sense of mission arises out of that view of reality. Furthermore, in the past, this view of reality drove our pioneers with a passion. In less than 100 years we carried an unpopular religion all over the world. Today, the worldwide church is baptizing one million new members every two-and-a-half years. The passion is still very much alive!

Not so much, however, in North America. I suspect that the demise of this vision among North American Adventists is due partly to the increased education of our people, which gives greater weight to other explanations of reality in our minds and tends to water down the importance of our religious sense of what really is and who we really are. Some Adventists today question whether our view of reality is any more valid than competing views of reality in other religious systems.

Many North American Adventists wish that Adventism on our continent could join the evangelism explosion that is occurring in other parts of the world. I am convinced that for this to happen in our part of the world, we must regain the vision of our pioneers, who believed, unshakably, that their view of truth and of world events was indeed the way things *really* are. We must regain the certainty that Ellen White affirmed, "We have the truth, we know it."[1] This view of reality must undergird our highest priorities and our most profound motives. Then, and only then, will North American Adventism join that of other parts of the world for what we historically have called "the glorious finishing of the work of God on the earth."

Unfortunately, such a view of reality is perceived by many people as presumptuous and snobbish. North America offers a smorgasbord of options from which consumers can pick and choose what suits them best, and we tend to extend this consumer mentality to religion. Each church or religion is thought to offer something good that someone, somewhere must surely need. No religion has a superior claim on truth, we are told. Whatever religion you choose as best for you, nothing more real is out there that you'd be better off choosing if only you knew about it.

This smorgasbord view of religion has a major weakness. If there is a God, and if His way of understanding the issues of life is *the* real way to understand them, then our search as humans should not be so much to pick and choose what suits us best, as to discover His will. I do not mean that we should try to get rid of the smorgasbord of options. That is what religious freedom—to which Adventists are so committed—is all about. What I mean is that we must not allow the smorgasbord of options to weaken our faith in the ultimate truthfulness of the Adventist view of reality. We must continue to interpret world events in light of the Adventist vision. And to do that, we must continually educate our people as to what that vision is. This is particularly critical today, because so many of us have never seen that vision.

Adventists share with many Christians the biblical view that Jesus Christ died for our sins, broke the bonds of death by His resurrection, and now lives in heaven as our Mediator. We agree that this is how things "really are." So what is unique about the Adventist view of reality? What do we teach that nobody else does, but which everyone needs to know?

The Adventist view of reality for today arises out of both the Bible and the writings of Ellen White. Biblically, the uniqueness of Adventism is our historical method of interpreting prophecy, by which we understand events in the world today. (I will discuss the historical method of prophetic interpretation in the next chapter.) We often say that the unique Adventist contribution to Christian theology is our understanding of the sanctuary. But our sanctuary theology arises directly out of our historical interpretation of prophecy. Daniel 8:14, without which there would be no sanctuary theology as we know it today, is both sanctuary and prophecy. Our sanctuary theology and our historical interpretation of prophecy rise and fall together. Others say that our unique contribution is the great controversy theme. This also is tied to prophecy, particularly the apocalyptic prophecies of Daniel and Revelation.

Added to our historical interpretation of Bible prophecy, and indeed as a continuation of it, is the witness of Ellen White, particularly her view of end-time events and how to prepare for them.

Seventh-day Adventists have always believed that the future as revealed by the historical method of interpreting Bible prophecy, and as expanded by Ellen White's views, is *the* realistic way to interpret world events today. It is the purpose

17

of this book to review the vision of reality that inspired our pioneers. I share that vision with the pioneers, and I hope that what I say here can help you to capture it—or recapture it. Whether you agree with every conclusion I draw in this book, I hope you will be challenged to think about your church and your relationship to God in new ways, and that from these new ways of thinking you will mature spiritually and be better prepared for the end time.

Before you begin the next chapter, I would like to tell you that it is a bit more difficult—heavier reading, we might say—than most of the rest of the book. However, chapter 2 is a very important part of the book because it helps us understand our own movement in the light of 2,000 years of prophetic interpretation. Skim the chapter if you find it difficult to understand. Skip the quoted material and pay attention to my own comments, particularly the material in boldface type. Later, when you have time, you can come back to the chapter for more thoughtful reading.

---

1. Ellen G. White, Letter 18, 1850.

One

The Great Advent Movement

CHAPTER

Two

The Historical Method of Interpreting Prophecy

I am not determined whether the Pope be Antichrist himself or only his apostle, so cruelly is Christ corrupted and crucified by him."[1]

So thundered Martin Luther nearly 500 years ago. And Protestant leaders all over Europe agreed.

"The Roman Pontiff, with his whole order and kingdom, is very Antichrist,"[2] said Philip Melanchthon, Luther's associate. And John Calvin affirmed that "the head of that cursed and abominable kingdom, in the Western Church, we affirm to be the Pope."[3]

The view that the pope (or the papacy) was the antichrist lay at the foundation of Reformation theology—so much so that the entire Protestant movement would have been vastly different had this view of the papacy been different. *And that is extremely significant to Seventh-day Adventists.*

The significance lies not so much in the conclusion itself as in the way it was reached—through the historical method of prophetic interpretation. According to the historical method of interpretation, the prophecies of Daniel begin with Babylon and continue in unbroken sequence to the second coming of

21

Christ. Most Adventists are familiar with Daniel's prophecies. We can diagram them along a time line like this:

Babylon	Medo-Persia	Greece	Rome	Divided Europe	Medieval Christianity	Judgment	Second Coming

For anyone familiar with Daniel's prophecies, the view that these prophecies continue in an unbroken sequence from Daniel's time to the second coming of Christ seems so obvious that one wonders how anyone could miss it. Actually, every prophetic interpreter I know of agrees that these prophecies extend from Babylon to Christ's coming. However, they do not all agree that these prophecies continue (1) in *unbroken* sequence (2) to the *second* coming of Christ. At least two other views exist. One states that the prophecies continue in a *broken* sequence to the second coming of Christ. The other view states that the prophecies continued to Christ's *first* coming.

The view that the prophecies continue in a *broken* sequence to the second coming of Jesus is called the *futurist* method of prophetic interpretation because it pushes the antichrist down to the end of time. Instead of identifying the little horn of Daniel 7 as the Christian church of the Middle Ages, it interprets the little horn as an evil power just before Christ's visible second coming. Note that there is a huge break of about 1,500 years between the division of Europe and the end time, and then—in order to get everything in—the little horn, the judgment, and the second coming are all bunched together like this:

Babylon	Medo-Persia	Greece	Rome	Divided Europe		Little Horn Judgment Second Coming
					—1500-year break—	

The futurist method of prophetic interpretation is by far the most popular view among conservative Protestants today. The rapture theory, popularized by Hal Lindsey's *The Late Great Planet Earth*, is based on this interpretation.

The other view of prophecy that differs from the historical method is called the *preterist* method of interpretation. According to preterists, the establishment of God's eternal kingdom was fulfilled at Christ's first coming, like this:

Babylon	Medo-Persia	Greece	Rome Divided Europe Little Horn Judgment Christ's Kingdom (first advent)

The problem with this view is that the last five items in the prophetic list must be jammed together in order to make the interpretation work. Actually, notice that in both the futurist and the preterist methods of interpretation, certain parts of the prophecy must be jammed together to make the interpretation fit. Without a doubt, the historical method is the most orderly, and the most reasonable, of these three ways of interpreting prophecy.

The Seventh-day Adventist view of end-time events, and particularly our view that the papacy will be reestablished as a major political power in the world at the end of time, is a continuation of the historical method of interpretation. It assures us that we are on the right track, in spite of the fact that almost the whole world has gone the other way. But where did the historical method for interpreting Daniel's prophecies come from? It actually goes back a long, long way.

Before the Christian era

On his march against the Persian Empire, Alexander the Great approached Jerusalem expecting a fight. To his surprise, the Jewish high priest opened the city gates and marched out to meet him dressed in his most sacred robes. When the astonished general asked why the Jews were sur-

23

rendering without a fight, the priest showed him Daniel's prophecy that foretold the overthrow of the Persian empire by a king of the Greeks. Alexander was so impressed that he offered sacrifices at the Jewish temple! This is clear evidence that long before Christ's time, the Jews correctly understood that part of Daniel's prophecy that applied to them.[4]

We find similar evidence in the Greek translation of the Old Testament. Actually, two editions, or versions, of the Greek translation of the Old Testament called the Septuagint (LXX) exist. The earliest version is quite interpretive and has long been rejected in favor of the more accurate Theodotian version. However, the earlier version provides us with a clear insight into the Jewish understanding of Daniel several centuries before Christ. Daniel 11:30 reads, "The ships of Chittim shall come against him" (KJV). For "ships of Chittim," the earlier, more interpretive version of the LXX says, "The *Romans* shall come and expel him [emphasis supplied]." Commenting on this, one authority says:

> The translator understood well one part, just that which a Jew, living at the time at Alexandria, would know. . . . He paraphrases rightly the words, "there shall come ships of Chittim," by, "And the Romans shall come and shall expel him."[5]

There is an important principle here:

God's people understood the part of the prophecy that applied to them at that time.

There is also evidence that the Jews anticipated Christ's first advent at the correct time.

Another significant interpretive translation of the earlier Septuagint is found in Daniel 9:25, where the sixty-two weeks are translated interpretively, "weeks of years." Says Froom:

> In this first interpretation of Daniel, giving mere flashes of third century B.C. prophetic understanding, the

24

first recorded exposition of time prophecy appears—the application concerning the "sixty-two of years (*sic*)" in the seventy weeks pertaining to the Jews, which if followed through would bring them face to face with the first advent and the suffering Messiah. . . . This prophetic exposition "of years," hints of the year-day principle, which was later to become an abiding heritage in the Christian Era, and never to be lost throughout succceeding centuries by either Jewish or Christian expositors.[6]

Froom points out that "there is definite evidence that about that time [A.D. 27] many Jews were looking for 'Messiah the Prince' to come."[7] Thus, Ellen White was essentially correct when she suggested that Christ's disciples were familiar with the seventy-week prophecy of Daniel 9:

The sixty-nine weeks were . . . to extend to "the Messiah the Prince," and with high hopes and joyful anticipations the disciples looked forward to the establishment of Messiah's kingdom at Jerusalem to rule over the whole earth.[8]

The disciples understood that the seventy-week prophecy pointed forward to the coming of the Messiah in their own time—a view shared by many at the time. Unfortunately, national pride kept them from correctly interpreting that part of the prophecy which said that Messiah was to be "cut off" in the midst of the seventieth week (Daniel 9:24), and thus they were deeply disappointed at Christ's death. However, again we see the principle:

God's people correctly understood the fulfillment of the seventy-week time prophecy because it applied to their time.

The early Christian era

We find a similar development during the first three or four hundred years after Christ. Students of Bible prophecy understood that the Roman Empire was to be broken into ten divi-

sions. Sometime between A.D. 150 and 200, the Christian
bishop Irenaeus wrote:

> In a still clearer light has John, in the Apocalypse,
> indicated to the Lord's disciples what shall happen in the
> last times, and concerning the ten kings who shall then
> arise, among whom the empire which now rules [the
> earth] shall be partitioned.[9]

Irenaeus correctly understood Daniel's (and John's) prediction of the breakup of the Roman Empire. He even mentioned ten divisions, or ten kings!

During the next 300 years, several of the major church
fathers followed this same line of prophetic interpretation.
Some of them even understood that the antichrist would arise
following the fall of Rome. However, it would have overwhelmed these prophetic interpreters to think that this antichrist was to rule for 1,260 *years*. They expected Christ's coming to be much sooner than that. Writing sometime between
A.D. 375 and 400, Jerome said:

> Antichrist is near whom the Lord Jesus Christ "shall
> consume with the spirit of His mouth." . . . Savage tribes
> in countless numbers have overrun all parts of Gaul. The
> whole country between the Alps and the Pyrenees, be-
> tween the Rhine and the Ocean, has been laid waste by
> hordes of Quadi, Vandals, Sarmatians, Alans, Gepids,
> Herules, Saxons, Bergundians, Allemanni, and—alas! for
> the commonweal!—even the Pannonians.[10]

Jerome's view clearly followed the historical method of
prophetic interpretation, which identifies the ten horns of
Daniel 7 as the barbarian nations that broke up the Roman
Empire and which places the rise of the antichrist immediately following Rome's collapse. Notice again that

**Jerome clearly understood the prophecies that
applied to his time.**

However, he failed to interpret correctly the 1,260 years which applied to a period much later.

The medieval period

The medieval period (A.D. 500-1500) brought a profound change in the way the Christian church as a whole interpreted prophecy. Augustine, one of the most influential Christian theologians of all time, taught that Christ fulfilled Daniel's prophecies about God's eternal kingdom by His *first* coming. As he understood it, Christ's kingdom of glory had already been established, and the church was that kingdom. (Notice the similarity between Augustine's view and the preterist method of interpretation.) This new interpretation of prophecy brought about a profound change in the way the church viewed itself. In his famous work *De civitate Dei (The City of God)* Augustine proposed that while the kingdom of God and the kingdoms of this world exist side by side at present, the kingdoms of this world are doomed to destruction, whereas the kingdom of God (the church) is eternal and will last forever. According to the *Encyclopedia Britannica*:

> During the first three centuries the eschatological views of the martyrs stood in the foreground. But since the time of the Roman emperor Constantine (died 337) the political recognition of Christianity has been understood as a realized hope in the Kingdom of Christ.[11]

Church leaders were happy enough to think of themselves as the rulers in God's eternal kingdom that had already come. The notion that the church, as the kingdom of God, would ultimately conquer the kingdoms of this world lay at the foundation of the church's grasp for political power during the Middle Ages. This resulted in the very abuses of power from the twelfth to the sixteenth centuries that Daniel had foretold. Augustine's distortion of Daniel's prophecies led directly to the fulfillment of those prophecies!

Augustine's view that Daniel's prophecy of God's eternal kingdom was fulfilled by the establishment of Christ's kingdom of grace at His first advent ruled out the idea that the ten horns and the little horn of Daniel 7 were fulfilled *after* that time. Says Leroy Froom of this period of Christian history:

> Men no longer looked to [historical] events for the fulfillment of the prophecies. The series of empires had already been passed, the stone kingdom of Daniel and the millennium of the Revelation were regarded as already in progress, and there was nothing yet in sight to fulfill the popular concept of the terrible Antichrist and his hordes of Gog and Magog. . . . The writers of prophetic exposition were . . . largely ignoring the historical meaning for the allegorical and spiritual application."[12]

Augustine's view prevailed for about a thousand years, causing people to lose sight of the prophecies of Daniel that foretold the end of the world. Why be bothered with what had already been fulfilled?

Pre-Reformation times

Protestants generally understand the Reformation to have begun about the year 1300 with John Wycliffe, a British scholar who translated the Bible into the English language. *It is extremely significant that prophecy began to be understood historically again at about this same time* (as opposed to Augustine's preterist method of interpretation). Once again, students of Bible prophecy understood the ten horns of Daniel 7 to be the barbarian tribes that took over the Roman Empire, and once again they understood that the antichrist was to follow. However, there was a difference. For the first time, interpreters of prophecy began to identify this antichrist as the church itself.

Also, about this time, students of prophecy began to apply the year-day principle to the 1260- and 2300-day prophecies. Joachim of Floris was the first to suggest that the 1260 days were, in reality, a prediction of 1260 years:

> There are 42 months or 1260 days, and they designate

nothing else than 1260 years, in which the mysteries of the New Testament consist.[13]

A Spanish physician, Arnold of Villanova (A.D. 1235-1313), interpreted the 2300 days of Daniel 8:14 to mean years:

When he says "two thousand three hundred days" it must be said that by days he understands years.[14]

Villanova went so far as to suggest that if one knew "how many years passed from the third year of Belshazzar to Christ, one could add the years from Christ to the present, and compute how many remain of the 2300 years until 'the year in which all generation and corruption will cease and time will be no longer.' "[15]

Shades of William Miller!

Who is the antichrist?

One of the most important conclusions of the modern historical method of interpretation is that the Catholic Church of the Middle Ages was the little horn of Daniel 7—the antichrist. Prior to Augustine's time, the view was almost universal that the antichrist would be a single individual, a Jew, who would rebuild the temple in Jerusalem. However, with the resurgence of the historical method at Wycliffe's time, this began to change. We shall now briefly trace the origin of the view that the papacy was the antichrist.

Eberhard II (A.D. 1200-1246), archbishop of Salzburg in the early 1200s, was apparently the first to take the view that the papacy was the antichrist. Said he:

Those priests [flamines] of Babylon alone desire to reign, they cannot tolerate an equal, they will not desist until they have trampled all things under their feet, and until they sit in the temple of God, and until they are exalted above all that is worshipped. . . . He who is servant of servants, desires to be lord of lords, just as if he were God. . . . He speaks great things as if he were truly God.

29

He ponders new counsels under his breast, in order that he may establish his own rule for himself, he changes laws, he ordains his own laws, he corrupts, he plunders, he pillages, he defrauds, he kills—that incorrigible man (whom they are accustomed to call Antichrist) on whose forehead an inscription of insult is written: "I am God, I cannot err." He sits in the temple of God, and has dominion far and wide. But as it is in the secrets of the holy writings, let him that readeth understand: the learned will understand, all the wicked will act wickedly, neither will they understand.[16]

While Eberhard does not mention either Daniel's prophecies or the papacy as their fulfillment, there can be no doubt that he had both in mind.

John Wycliffe (A.D. 1324-1384), an eminent scholar and professor at Oxford University, lived during a time when two rival popes claimed Peter's chair, each pronouncing the other antichrist. Wycliffe was utterly outspoken in his denunciation of the papacy as the antichrist, the little horn of Daniel 7:

Why is it necessary in unbelief to look for another Antichrist? Hence in the seventh chapter of Daniel Antichrist is forcefully described by a horn arising in the time of the fourth kingdom, . . . having eyes and a mouth speaking great things against the Lofty One, and wearing out the saints of the Most High, and thinking that he is able to change times and laws. For so our clergy foresee the lord pope, as it is said of the eighth blaspheming little head.[17]

Please notice that:

Wycliff and others at his time correctly understood the prophecy about the little horn of Daniel 7 because it applied to their time.

The Reformation period

It is common knowledge that the Protestant Reformation was established on the foundational plank of righteousness by faith. What is not so well known is that *prophecy interpreted according to the historical method* formed another plank on which the Reformation was founded. The view that the pope was the antichrist, which began as a trickle about the time of Wycliffe, became a torrent by the time of Martin Luther.

For several hundred years, students of Bible prophecy had been calling the pope the antichrist. At first, Luther had no intention of establishing another religious organization. He entered upon his opposition to the papacy intending only to reform the church. His discovery that this was impossible led him to accept the view that the papacy was the antichrist. *Without the prophetic understanding that the papacy was the antichrist, Luther would not have been impelled to establish a religious movement separate from the Church of Rome.* Protestants owe much more than they realize—and even more than most Adventists realize—to the Reformers' understanding of prophecy, which, interpreted historically, states that the papacy is the antichrist. Says Leroy Froom:

> Literally hundreds of volumes or tractates were written in the contest of Protestant and Catholic pens [during the Reformation] regarding the charge that the Papacy was the predicted Antichrist, with its allotted time fast expiring. It was the profound conviction springing from the great outline prophecies, and the inescapable conclusion that the Papacy was the predicted Antichrist, that impelled separation and gave courage to battle the great apostasy. [18]

It would be impossible for us, in this short survey, to review this literature in any depth, so I will quote representative statements:

> *Martin Luther, German Reformer*: "That true Antichrist mentioned by St. Paul reigns in the court of Rome and is, as I think I can prove, a greater pest than the Turks." [19]

31

Ulrich Zwingli, Swiss Reformer: "I know that in it [the papacy] works the might and power of the Devil, that is, of the Antichrist."[20]

William Tyndale, British Reformer: "And [they] have set up that great idol, the whore of Babylon, antichrist of Rome, whom they call pope.[21]

John Calvin, French Reformer: "Daniel and Paul had predicted that Antichrist would sit in the temple of God. The head of that cursed and abominable kingdom, in the Western Church, we affirm to be the Pope."[22]

Notice the principle once again:

The reformers understood Daniel's little-horn prophecy to have been fulfilled in their day because it applied to their time.

A growing understanding of the 1260 days

As the time approached for the 1260- and 2300-day prophecies to reach their end, students of prophecy understood their significance more and more clearly. About a hundred years after Luther, the English theologian George Downham (died A.D. 1634) identified the little horn of Daniel 7 as the papacy *and interpreted the 1260-day prophecy as 1260 years, beginning in the time of Justinian, from about A.D. 600 " 'according to the round number.' "[23]

The British clergyman Drue Cressener (A.D. 1638-1718) was the first Bible student to identify correctly the actual dates for the 1260-year prophecy:

The first appearance of the Beast was at *Justinians* recovery of the *Western* Empire, from which time to about the year 1800 will be about 1260 years.[24]

Cressener's understanding of the little horn was remarkably close to the view held by Adventists today. He recognized, correctly, that the time, times, and half a time had to begin *after* the division of the Roman Empire by the barbarian tribes:

> For if the first time of the Beast was at *Justinians* recovery of the City of *Rome*, then must not it end till a little before the year 1800.[25]

And "a little before the year 1800" is exactly when the period of papal supremacy ended! Cressener was right on target—and just when he should have been. He died in 1718, just eighty years before the actual fulfillment of the prophecy in 1798.

As the time for the fulfillment of the 1260-day prophecy drew near, Bible expositors increasingly anticipated not only the correct date but also France as the agent that would bring about the end of papal power. One of these was Thomas Newton (A.D. 1704-1782), who said:

> Rome therefore will finally be destroyed by some of the princes, who are reformed, or shall be reformed from popery: and as the kings of France have contributed greatly to her advancement, it is not impossible, nor improbable, that some time or other they may also be the principal authors of her destruction. France hath already shown some tendency towards a reformation, and therefore may appear more likely to effect such a revolution.[26]

As all students of history know, the French Revolution, which occurred between 1790 and 1795, precipitated the fall of the papacy.

In 1796 the London *Evangelical Magazine* published two articles by George Bell entitled, "The Downfall of Antichrist," which Bell had written in 1795. Bell predicted the fall of antichrist in either 1797 or 1813:

> If this be a right application of events to the prophecy, then Antichrist arose about the year 537, or at farthest about the year 553. He continues 42 months, or 1260

prophetical days, that is, 1260 years, Rev. xiii.5; consequently we may expect his fall about the year 1797, or 1813.[27]

Another magazine, the London *Baptist Annual Register*, published a remarkable article written by an American clergyman on March 31, 1798:

> We are not able so accurately to fix the meaning of those prophecies, that are now about to be accomplished, as we shall easily do a few years hence. However, I cannot help thinking, that Rome will soon fall into the hands of the French, and that the Pope will be deprived of all his temporal dominions; that is, that he will soon cease to be a beast . . . which I apprehend is nigh at hand, and, *perhaps, will be accomplished before this letter can reach Great Britain.* The Pope, being deprived of his temporalities, will be nothing but a false prophet, and then the seventh trumpet will sound.[28]

Please notice: The pope was taken prisoner between February 15 and 20, 1798. The American author of the statement quoted above, writing on March 31, had not yet learned of this momentous event and, writing some six weeks after the event, "predicted" that it would occur at the hands of the French, as indeed it already had! Notice again that shortly before 1798:

Students of prophecy recognized the end of the 1260 days because this prophecy applied to their time.

A growing understanding of the 2300 days

To Seventh-day Adventists, the most important biblical time prophecy is the 2300 days, or years, of Daniel 8:14. We understand that this prophecy began in 457 B.C. concurrently with the seventy weeks and that it ended in 1844. We shall give our attention during the remainder of this chapter to a brief survey of how this understanding of the 2300 days came about.

Johann Funck (A.D. 1518-1566). Johann Funck, a German clergyman who was a few years younger than Luther, was apparently the first reformer to correctly date the seventy weeks of Daniel 9:24 between 457 B.C. and A.D. 34. It was common at that time to begin the seventy-week prophecy at Daniel's own time, about 100 years before 457. Funck took exception to this view in words that are very familiar to Adventist students of prophecy:

> In the time of Cyrus [Daniel's time], only the temple was built, and the religious worship was arranged to some degree. . . . However, when Ezra received the order and the authority to install judges and magistrates, . . . [then] began the building of the town of Jerusalem and of the nation of Judea. . . . Therefore I consider this year, which was the seventh of Darius Artaxerxes Longimanus, the beginning of the seventy weeks of Daniel.[29]

Jacques Cappel (A.D. 1570-1624). About fifty years later, the French theologian and historian Jacques Cappel recognized 457 B.C. as the beginning of the seventy weeks and the baptism of Christ as the end of the sixty-nine weeks:

> The weeks are to begin with the publishing of the edict of Artaxerxes Longimanus [457 B.C.], an edict obtained by Ezra in the seventh year of his reign. . . . Therefore, from that edict to the baptism of our Lord, who by the voice of the Father was declared the Christ and the Prince of our salvation, there are sixty-nine entire weeks.[30]

Sir Isaac Newton (A.D. 1642-1727). Many people are not aware that Sir Isaac Newton, one of the greatest scientists of all time, was also a keen student of Bible prophecy. Newton also correctly dated the beginning of the seventy weeks:

> *Seventy weeks are cut out upon thy people, and upon thy holy city, to finish transgression, &c.* Here, by putting a week for seven years, are reckoned 490 years from the

time that the dispersed *Jews* should be re-incorporated into a people and a holy city, until the death and resurrection of Christ. . . .

Now the dispersed *Jews* became a people and city when they first returned into a polity or body politick; and this was in the seventh year of *Artaxerxes Longimanus*.[31]

Johann Petri (A.D. 1718-1792). The 2300-day prophecy provides no information as to its beginning or end. The key to finding the correct date is to recognize the close relationship between Daniel 8 and Daniel 9 and to begin the 2300 days at the same time as the seventy weeks. The first student of prophecy to make this connection was the German theologian Johann Petri. The angel told Daniel to seal up the prophecy till the time of the end, because it would not be understood until that time. Is it not significant that Petri discovered the key to understanding the 2300 days less than 100 years before the time for its fulfillment in 1844? Said he:

And therefore, I find that the commentators up to now could not possibly understand the vision, because they separated the second vision Dan. 8 and 9 [the seventy weeks from the 2300 days]. It is impossible to cut off one piece of this vision and then to understand the whole of it without its [proper] connections. Therefore such commentators neither could find the beginning nor the end of the seventy weeks.[32]

Commenting on Petri's landmark discovery, Froom says:

The significance of the Petri contribution looms before us in its true proportions in the light of the following retrospect: The year-day principle, as applied to the 70 weeks by the Jews centuries before Christ, was generally accepted by Christians; next was added the application of the principle to the 1260 days by Joachim, about A.D. 1190. This, in turn, was extended to the 2300 days by Villanova about 1297 and Cusa in 1440—dating its beginning from the time of the vision. During the Reformation men like Funck (1564) were perfecting the chronology of the 70 weeks, which was generally connected with the death of Christ, but as yet unconnected with the 2300 years. . . .

And now Petri, in 1768, evidently was the first to begin these related greater and lesser periods together; he began both periods 453 years before Christ's birth, with the cross in the midst of the seventieth week, and ended the longer period in the year 1847 after Christ's birth.[33]

Alexander Campbell. One of America's important religious leaders during the first half of the nineteenth century was Alexander Campbell, who established the Disciples of Christ. Campbell used the seventy weeks to prove that Christ came at the time appointed by prophecy and then connected the seventy weeks with the 2300 days:

> Daniel then fixes the time of the nativity; the commencement of the kingdom, or confirmation of the covenant, and the ultimate cleansing of the sanctuary, or purgation of the Christian church from antichristian abominations. This last event was to be two thousand three hundred years from the aforesaid date. That is, from the birth of Jesus about eighteen hundred and forty-seven years.[34]

Beginning about 1800, and for the next fifty years, the view that the 2300 days were about to end literally exploded. Froom lists 132 men between 1800 and 1840 who taught that the 2300 years would end sometime during the nineteenth century. Of these, 113 gave dates between 1843 and 1847, and most of them preferred 1843.[35] Again, early in the nineteenth century:

Students of prophecy understood that the 2300 days were about to be fulfilled because this prophecy applied to their time.

This concludes our review of the development of the historical method of interpretation. There are two points I hope you picked up from this study:

1. **God's people during history always understood that part of the prophecies applied to their own time, and this understanding often began to emerge two hundred years or more prior to the actual fulfillment of the prophecy.**

2. **Growth in the understanding of prophecy was a collective effort by the entire body of Christ throughout Christian history, not by just a few people in one age.**

If you are wondering why I gave you this quick review of prophetic interpretation during the Christian era, keep reading. It will immediately become apparent to you.

---

1. Martin Luther, *Schriften*, vol. 21a, col. 156 (Froom, II:254).

2. Philip Melanchthon, *Disputationes*, No. 56, "De Matrimonio," in *Opera (Corpus Reformatorum)*, vol. 12, col. 535 (Froom, II:288).

3. John Calvin, *Institutes*, vol. 2, p. 314 (Froom, II:437).

4. The source for this incident is Josephus, a Jewish historian (A.D. 37 to 100) whom modern historians feel is not reliable in this instance. However, for our purposes it does not matter whether the event actually happened. What matters is that the Jews at Josephus' time, and no doubt for scores if not hundreds of years before, understood Daniel's male goat (Daniel 8:5-8) to have been fulfilled by Alexander the Great and the Greek Empire. See Froom, I:167-169.

5. E. B. Pusey, *Daniel the Prophet*, 377 (Froom, I:175).

6. Froom, I:175, 176.

7. Froom, I:145.

8. Ellen G. White, *The Great Controversy*, p. 345.

9. Irenaeus, *Against Heresies*, book 5, chap. 26, pp. 554, 555 (Froom, I:245).

10. Jerome, Letter 123 (to Ageruchia), in *Nicene and Post Nicene Fathers*, 2nd series, vol. 6, pp. 236, 237 (Froom, I:445).

11. *Encyclopaedia Britannica*, fifteenth edition, vol. 6, p. 962-c.

12. Froom, I:900, 901.

13. Joachim of Floris, *Concordia*, vol. 118 r (Froom I:712).

14. Translated from Arnold of Villanova, *Introductio in Librum*

[Joachim] De Semine, vol. 7 v, col. 2, line 34 to vol. 8 r, col. 1, line 2 (Froom I:750).

15. Villanova, *Tractatus . . . Antichristi*, vol. 61 r, col. 1, lines 11-24 (Froom, I:752, 753).

16. Translated from Ioannas Aventinus, *Annales Boiorum Libri Septem*, p. 684 (Froom, I:800).

17. Translated from John Wycliffe, *De Veritate Sacrae Scripturae*, vol. 3, pp. 267, 268 (Froom, II:55).

18. Froom, II:245.

19. Martin Luther, *Dr. Martin Luthers Sämmtliche Schriften* (edited by Johann Georg Walch), vol. 15, col. 2430 (Froom, II:253).

20. Ulrich Zwingli, *Hauptschriften*, vol. 7, p. 135 (Froom, II:335).

21. William Tyndale, *The Obedience of a Christian Man*, in *Works*, vol. 1, p. 191 (Froom, II:356).

22. John Calvin, *Institutes*, vol. 2, p. 314 (Froom, II:437).

23. Froom, II:536.

24. Drue Cressener, *The Judgments of God Upon the Roman Catholick Church*, p. 309 (Froom, II:596).

25. *Ibid*, p. 312.

26. Thomas Newton, *Dissertations on the Prophecies* (2nd ed.), vol. 3, p. 308 (Froom: II:724).

27. George Bell, *The Evangelical Magazine*, 1796, vol. 4, p. 54 (Froom, II:742).

28. *Baptist Annual Register*, January 1799, p. 144, italics in the original (Froom, II:743, 744).

29. Translated from Johann Funk, *Ausslegung*, sig. H5r (Froom, II:312).

30. Jacques Cappel, *Les livrées de Babel, ou l' histoire du sièqe romain*, p. 1005 (Froom, II:632).

31. Sir Isaac Newton, *Observations*, pp. 130, 131 italics in Froom (Froom, II:662).

32. Johann Petri, *Gründlicher Beweis*, p. 15 (Froom, II:718).

33. Froom, II:718.

34. Alexander Campbell, *Debate on the Evidences of Christianity . . . Between Robert Owen . . . and Alexander Campbell*, vol. 2, p. 74 (Froom, IV:253).

35. See charts by L. E. Froom in *Prophetic Faith of Our Fathers*, vol. 3, pp. 744, 745, and vol. 4, pp. 404, 405; 846, 847.

Three

Prophetic Significance of the Millerite Movement

W as William Miller led by God? Was God the moving force behind the Millerite movement that reached its climax on October 22, 1844? For nearly 150 years Seventh-day Adventists have answered that question with a resounding *Yes*. That has been our view of reality.

However, during the last half of the twentieth century a change has come within the church. Today, a significant number of skeptics among Seventh-day Adventists themselves claim that God was *not* behind the Millerite movement, and that the 1844 disappointment was a sad mistake. According to this view, the historic Adventist teachings about Christ's change of ministry in the heavenly sanctuary and about the investigative judgment are simply face-saving devices which the church adopted because it could not admit that the Millerites were wrong.

It was not just the *event* that was to take place in 1844 that Miller and his followers are said to have misunderstood. Their error, we are told, was in thinking that Daniel 8:14 said anything at all about 1844. Miller was, after all, a farmer, not a theologian, and it is a mistake to base our understanding of how things really are on his interpretation of prophecy.

I can not prove, in any scientific sense, that God was behind the Millerite movement and the establishment of the Seventh-day Adventist Church. I have not discussed this matter personally with God or any other heavenly being, and even if I had, people would as soon (and probably sooner!) disbelieve me as they would Ellen White, the one person in Adventism who claimed to have discussed the matter with a representative from God. Short of God's giving a divine revelation to every human being—or at least to every Adventist—nobody can prove to anyone else that God directed in the establishment of the Seventh-day Adventist Church. Anyone who is going to base his view of reality on that premise must do so by faith.

However, our faith does not have to be blind. While there is no absolute proof, there are certainly logical evidences that God was at work. It is these evidences that I want to examine in this chapter and the next. I will share with you the reasons why it makes sense to me that God was behind the Millerite movement. You must evaluate what I say for yourself.

The historical method of interpretation

One of the most important points to keep in mind as we evaluate Miller's movement is that it was a direct outgrowth of the historical method of interpretation. Indeed, the Millerite movement was the logical conclusion toward which the historical method of interpretation had been tending, though nobody realized this prior to the nineteenth century. Please do not think that this was the only way Christians interpreted prophecy from the time of Christ to Miller's day. We have already noted that the historical method, which developed quite strongly during the first 400 years of Christian history, all but died out during the Middle Ages. If the historical method of interpreting Daniel and Revelation is the one God had in mind when He gave the prophecies—and I believe it was—then it was simply another of those teachings of the Bible that was distorted by the papacy during its long supremacy, along with salvation, the Sabbath, man's nature in death, the punishment of the wicked, and a host of others.

But with the Reformation came a restoration of the historical method of interpretation. You will recall that the restoration of the truth about righteousness by faith was one of two teachings that gave power to the Protestant Reformation. The other was the view, derived from the historical method of interpretation, that the papacy was the antichrist.[1]

So in responding to the question of whether the Millerite movement was of God, we must ask ourselves whether the historical method of prophetic interpretation was of God. It is helpful, in evaluating this, to go further and ask whether the Protestant Reformation came about through God's direction. To any true Protestant, the answer is obviously Yes. Was the Protestant view during the Reformation, that the papacy was the antichrist, of God? I don't see how we can escape that conclusion. This view is not very popular today. Most Protestants find it rather embarrassing and would just as soon forget about it. But the fact is that *there would have been no Reformation without the view that the papacy was the antichrist.* All the Reformers' efforts would have been directed at changing the church from within. There would have been no impetus to break with the Catholic Church and establish a new religious movement. Whether they like it today or not, I don't see how Protestants can escape this important conclusion.

If the historical method of interpretation was one of the two teachings that fueled the Reformation, which I think most evangelical Protestants agree was directed by God, and if it formed the basis of the Millerite movement; if, in fact, the Millerite movement was the logical end point toward which the historical method had wittingly or unwittingly been leading all along, then it seems to me that we have gone a long way toward answering our question about whether the Millerite movement was from God.

When was prophecy to be unsealed?

The angel told Daniel that nobody would understand the 2300-day prophecy till the time of the end (see Daniel 8:26). Only two explanations of the 2300 days have gained any degree of acceptance. One is the Antiochus Epiphanes theory, and the other is the view that the 2300 days ended in 1844.[2] The Jews before Christ were the first to suggest that Daniel 8:11-14 predicted Antiochus's attack on Jerusalem and the temple in 165 B.C., and this view has been adopted by some Christians from the early church to the present. In fact, I am no doubt safe in saying that the vast majority of Bible interpreters today, both preterists and futurists, accept the Antiochus Epiphanes theory.

A number of valid reasons exist for rejecting this view, but it would exceed the scope of this book to discuss them here. I will bring up just one point: If the 2300-day prophecy was not to be understood till the end time, then I have no difficulty rejecting an interpretation that was first proposed almost before the ink was dry on Daniel's scroll![3]

Contrast this with the view adopted by Miller in 1818. We have already noted in the previous chapter that this was not just Miller's view. Scores—perhaps hundreds—of other students of prophecy reached the same conclusion at about the same time. It is a well-documented fact that a worldwide movement began about the year 1800 whose major premise was that the second coming of Christ was very near. The impetus for this preaching was based on the prophecies of Daniel and Revelation—and particularly on Daniel's prophecies of the 1260 days and the 2300 days. To this day thousands—indeed millions—besides Seventh-day Adventists still preach the imminent return of Christ. This *is* the end time. The interpretation of the 2300-day prophecy adopted by Miller and hundreds of others during the first half of the nineteenth century came at the time of the end—exactly when the angel told Daniel that this prophecy would be understood.

I repeat, when there are just two interpretations of a prophecy, one ancient and the other very recent, and when the angel said that the prophecy would not be understood till the time of the end, which view will you choose? I don't have much trouble making the choice.

And now to get back to our original question. Did God lead in the advent movement of the early nineteenth century? Are we, in the closing years of the twentieth century, safe in basing our view of reality on that premise? If there is proof of this point, then to me, the reasons that I have just presented are among the strongest evidences that the answer to that question is a positive *Yes*:

1. **The advent movement leading up to 1844 was the climax of two millenniums of the historical interpretation of Bible prophecy—an interpretation that, together with the doctrine of righteousness by faith, fueled the Protestant Reformation 300 years earlier.**
2. **The Millerite movement came at exactly the right time in history to fulfill the angel's prediction to Daniel that nobody would understand his visions, particularly the 2300-day prophecy of Daniel 8:14, till the time of the end.**

However, before reaching a final conclusion regarding God's part in the Millerite movement, we must examine the movement itself and the man behind it.

---

1. For a more complete discussion of this view, see L. E. Froom, II:243-245.

2. A third view gained some prominence prior to William Miller's time: that the little horn of Daniel 8:10-12 was Islam. This view died with the Millerite movement and has not been revived since. (See P. Gerard Damsteegt, *Foundations of the Seventh-day Adventist Message and Mission*, p. 30, 57-60; L. E. Froom, *The Prophetic Faith of Our Fathers*, charts in vol. 4, pp. 396, 397; 404, 405.)

3. Figuratively speaking. Daniel wrote this prophecy between 550 and 540 B.C., several hundred years before the time of Antiochus Epiphanes.

Four

William Miller and His Movement

I t is impossible to separate the movements God has initiated in the history of our world from the men He used to initiate them. The movement is not only the man, but the kind of man. It is not only the call, but the circumstances in the man's life from which the call arises.

Two factors stand out in God's call of the apostle Paul. First, he was an extremely intense person. When something mattered, it mattered all the way. You and I would have recoiled in shock at the suggestion that Saul be the Lord's banner bearer to the Gentiles. But God knew better. The fact that Saul was fighting on the wrong side did not matter to Him. Saul burned with passion for his cause. God could more easily take a man with a fire inside and turn him around than He could start a fire in someone who didn't have one burning in his soul to start with. Intensity of purpose seems to be one of God's qualifications for great spiritual leadership. There is no revival without it.

The second thing God seems to look for in His choice of a strong spiritual leader is a crisis of faith. It seems quite likely that for some time before God called him on the road to

Damascus, Saul probably struggled with his conscience, tormented by the nagging thought that these Christians might be right after all. But his theological presuppositions could not allow that, so he pursued the Christians more fiercely.

When God met him on the Damascus road, he was ready. From that point on he was as utterly a disciple *for* Jesus as he had been opposed to Him before. A man whose convictions ran deep, whose beliefs were always profound, he was exactly the kind of person God could use.

We find the same characteristics in Martin Luther, another great religious leader, who was the moving force behind a powerful spiritual revolution.

Luther faced a deep crisis of faith. He was plagued by doubts about his personal religious life, about his worthiness before God. He resolved that crisis through the study of the Word. A man of powerful convictions, he was utterly unshakable after that. Luther was never chained to the stake. He never stood before a firing squad. But we need not entertain any doubts that he would have faced death a hundred times rather than yield his convictions.

These twin characteristics—a crisis of faith, and unshakable convictions following the resolution of that crisis—made Paul, Luther, and many other men the great spiritual leaders that they were. Great spiritual movements do not happen in a vacuum. If we want to understand God's leading in a movement, we must understand His leading in the lives of its movers and shakers. One of the greatest evidences of God's direction in a movement is His leading in the lives of the men and women at its head.

It has been estimated that 100,000 people had joined the Millerite movement by late 1844.[1] The United States had a population of twenty million at the time. Today's American population is twelve times what it was in 1844. A modern revival would have to bring in 1.2 million souls to equal the impact on the American population of the Millerite movement of the 1840s. The advent movement leading up to 1844 was a powerful spiritual revival.

What kind of man was behind it?

William Miller and his call

Miller was brought up in a Christian home. A voracious reader, he sometimes arose late at night to read by the fire. Several influential neighbors made their libraries available to him—a judge and a congressman among them. Unfortunately, after reading Voltaire and Paine and associating with deists in his community, Miller gave up religion and professed to be a deist.

During the War of 1812 Miller was commissioned a captain in the United States Army. Two years of military service caused him to recognize the emptiness of the deist philosophy. Settling on a 200-acre farm in Low Hampton, New York, after his discharge, he determined to find out the truth about God for himself.

Miller's activities during the next two years clearly suggest that his experience as a deist was a time of profound religious turmoil, when, like the apostle Paul, he outwardly professed one thing but apparently harbored serious internal reservations. Reflecting on this time in his life, he later wrote:

> The heavens were as brass over my head, and the earth as iron under my feet. *Eternity!—what was it? And death—why was it?* The more I reasoned, the further I was from demonstration. The more I thought, the more scattered were my conclusions. I tried to stop thinking, but my thoughts would not be controlled. I was truly wretched, but did not understand *the cause*. I murmured and complained, but knew not of whom. I knew that there was a wrong, but knew not how or where to find the right. I mourned, but without hope.[2]

Miller began attending church sporadically, occasionally reading the sermon when the minister was absent from the pulpit. On one occasion, he read a sermon from *Proudfit's Practical Sermons* on Isaiah 53. So moved was he by the sense of God's love and the great sacrifice the Father and the Son made for lost sinners that he was compelled to sit down, weep-

49

ing. Thoroughly converted, Miller determined to give himself completely to the study of the Bible in order to find the answers to his questions.

Now his love for reading and study stood him in good stead. For the next two years he devoted himself to the study of the Bible, literally day and night. Taking as his only aid for study *Cruden's Concordance* and certain history books, he determined to read through the Bible only as fast as his questions were satisfactorily answered. His agnostic friends laughed at him, but this only increased his determination to find the answers for himself. As he studied the prophecies, he became convicted that they spoke of his own time. At the end of two years, he reached a startling conclusion, based on the 2300-day prophecy of Daniel 8:14:

> I was thus brought, in 1818, . . . to the solemn conclusion, that in about twenty-five years from that time [1818] all the affairs of our present state would be wound up.[3]

Miller was so overwhelmed by the implication of what he had learned that he at first could not believe it. Determined to settle the question, he spent the next four years reviewing every point, raising every possible objection to his conclusions, and searching for the answers. On September 22, 1822, he composed a personal statement of twenty points that he called, "Compendium of Faith." Article 15 states: "I believe that the second coming of Jesus Christ is near, even at the door, even within twenty-one years—on or before 1843."[4]

For nine more years Miller refined his views. By 1831 he felt utterly convicted that he should share with others the news that Jesus was about to return. At first he spoke his convictions privately. However, he could not shake the conviction that he should do more than just witness privately to friends. Froom tells the story of the climax of this struggle:

> Miller's deepening distress and inward struggle of conscience over his duty to tell his convictions to the world

came to a climax one eventful summer's day in 1831. . . . The conviction came to his mind with greater urgency than ever before, "Go and tell it to the world." It was just as if God had spoken the words. The impression was so realistic and so powerful that he sank back into his well-worn chair and entered into an actual colloquy about the matter. "I can't go, Lord," he said. "Why not?" seemed to come the answering question.

Miller marshaled all the old threadbare excuses that he could summon—about his age [he was fifty at the time], not being a preacher, his lack of training, want of ability, slowness of speech, and the like. But not one of them, or all of them together, could silence the voice of conviction that insisted it was his bounden obligation to share his faith with others in a public way. His distress of soul became so great that he entered then and there into a solemn covenant with God, sealed with prayer, that if God definitely opened the way he would go and perform his duty to the world. "What do you mean by opening the way?" the voice seemed to ask. "Why," he replied, "if I should have an invitation to speak publicly in any place, I will go and tell them what I have found."[5]

Miller relaxed, satisfied that the matter was finally settled. Nobody would ever ask *him* to preach on prophecy. Half an hour later there came a knock at the front door. Answering it, Miller discovered his nephew, Irving Guilford, on the porch. "Our minister is away," the lad said. "He cannot preach next Sunday. Father asked me to come over and invite you to share with us your convictions on the second coming of Christ."

Miller was stunned. "I rebelled at once against the Lord, and determined not to go," he later wrote.[6] Leaving the boy standing in his front room without an answer, he stormed out of the house and down to a maple grove nearby.

The struggle was intense. He had come to that crucial moment of decision that comes to many a life that is moved by deep conviction. In the shadows of the maple grove, hard by his home, Miller fell to his knees and first prayed that God would release him from his promise. But the only answer he seemed to receive was the now familiar, "Go and tell it to the world." . . . Then and there upon his knees, he surrendered to the clear mandate of God, and said, "Lord, I will go."[7]

That is the story of William Miller's call—a call that thirteen years later would so stir the American nation that 100,000 people would respond to his message. I ask you, Did God really call William Miller? Is his personal experience valid evidence of God's direction in the movement that sprang up during succeeding years?

The movement itself

I have already mentioned that by mid to late 1844 some 100,000 people had accepted Miller's teaching. But what was the character of the movement? Is there evidence in the movement itself that can help us answer the question, Was God behind it all?

When a movement is of God, man does not have to push and shove to make it work. Three thousand were converted to Christ on the day of Pentecost, and Christianity spread rapidly throughout Judea and Samaria after that. Similarly, the Protestant movement spread rapidly beyond Luther and Wittenberg. No more than a few weeks after Luther posted his ninety-five theses on the church door in Wittenberg (October 31, 1517), copies had been distributed all over Germany. Within four years Lutheranism had "assumed the proportions of a national movement."[8] Within sixty years of Luther's revolt, the religious map of Europe was transformed to about its present boundaries.

One of the chief characteristics of a movement that is from God is that it is pushed along by forces that go far beyond what one man or even a group of men could do alone.

How was it with the Millerite movement?

We have already seen how Miller obtained his first appointment to preach the prophecies. When he returned home on Monday, he found in his mail a letter from an Elder Fuller, pastor of a Baptist church in Poultney, Vermont, asking him to preach the second coming and the prophecies to his congregation. Miller himself wrote of his preaching immediately after that:

> From thence (Poultney) I went by invitation to Powlet and other towns in that vicinity. The churches of Congregationalists, Baptists and Methodists were thrown open. In almost every place I visited, my labors resulted in the reclaiming of backsliders, and the conversion of sinners. . . . The most pressing invitations from the ministry, and the leading members of the churches poured in continually, from that time, during the whole period of my public labors, and with more than one half of which I was unable to comply. Churches were thrown open every where, and I lectured to crowded houses, through the western part of Vermont, the northern part of New York, and in Canada East. And powerful reformations were the results of my labors.[9]

For the next two years Miller continued to maintain his farm and his duties as justice of the peace in Hampton. However, in late 1834, following the fall harvest, he turned his farm over to his sons and from then on devoted his life fully to preaching. From 1832 to 1844, he gave 3200 sermons and lectures!

For five years, from 1834 to 1839, Miller preached largely in rural communities. However, in November 1839, he met Joshua Himes, a Boston minister of the Christian Connection denomination, who asked him why he had not preached in the large cities. Miller replied that he never preached anywhere that he was not invited, whereupon Himes told Miller to "prepare for a great campaign—that the doors would be opened in every State in the Union east of the Mississippi. And this erelong was literally fulfilled—beyond Miller's fondest expectations at that time."[10]

Himes became Miller's manager and publisher. "In many ways Himes was the leading figure in the Millerite movement—a human dynamo of energy, ever pushing the cause of publishing and preaching, and organizing the various enterprises connected with the movement."[11] Soon hundreds of ministers were preaching the Adventist message, including some of the leading Protestant clergymen of the day, among them Dr. Henry Dana Ward, Episcopal rector of St. Jude's Church in New York City.

From 1842 to 1844 some forty Adventist magazines, newspapers, and journals began publication, from Canada to Washington, D.C., and from New York to Cincinnati. Sixteen general conferences of Millerite leaders were held in various locations throughout the region. The Broadway Tabernacle in New York City, with a seating capacity of 3,500, was filled, and the Chinese Museum in Philadelphia, which accommodated 5,000, was "packed to suffocation."[12]

One of the questions these leaders struggled with was how to get the message of the soon coming of Jesus to the masses of the people. Camp meetings seemed to be the solution. The first camp meeting was held in Hatley, Quebec, in the summer of 1842. One of the ministers, Josiah Litch, reported that "waves on waves of people have flowed in upon us, day after day, until our arena within the circle of the tents has been almost crowded with a living mass of beings, eagerly enquiring, 'Watchman, what of the night?' "[13]

A hundred were converted at that camp meeting and five to six hundred at a second camp meeting in nearby Bolton a few weeks later. The first camp meeting in the United States, at East Kingston, New Hampshire, drew crowds numbering as high as 10,000! Thirty-one camp meetings were held the following summer (1843), and 130 camp meetings were held between 1843 and 1844.[14] To accommodate the crowds, a huge tent was purchased that would seat up to 4,000 persons. It was the largest tent in the United States at that time, yet even it proved to be too small, and a forty-foot splice was added, increasing the seating capacity to 6,000.

The year 1843 passed, and Jesus had not yet come. Still, most of the leaders of the Advent movement continued preaching the soon return of Christ. However, few of them were prepared for a turn of events that began with the Exeter, New Hampshire, camp meeting that was held August 12-17, 1844.

Samuel Snow, an Adventist preacher who had devoted a great deal of time to the study of the yearly feast days of the Jews, noted that Jesus died on the *very day* of the Passover Feast in A.D. 31—and His death was a fulfillment of the Passover. The outpouring of the Holy Spirit occurred on the *very day* of the Jewish feast of Pentecost, of which it was a fulfillment. The Passover and Pentecost, in the spring of the year, were types of the events surrounding Christ's first coming. Snow reasoned that the feasts in the autumn of the Jewish year, which were types of the events surrounding Christ's second coming, should also be fulfilled on the *very day* of their occurrence in the Jewish calendar. Since the Day of Atonement in the year 1844 fell on October 22, Snow declared that Jesus would return on that day, in just a few weeks.

The response to Snow's announcement was electrifying. Debts were paid. Sins were confessed. Wrongs were righted. Farmers left their potatoes unharvested in the fields. Merchants closed their shops, mechanics left their trade, teachers resigned their posts. The message "flew as it were upon the wings of the wind."[15]

Many of the Adventist leaders—Miller, Litch, Himes, and others—were reluctant at first to accept the specific date, October 22. However, compelled by the uncontrollable force with which the movement spread, they all eventually accepted the exact time.

Like a tidal wave the movement swept over the land. . . . Fanaticism disappeared before this proclamation like early frost before the rising sun. Believers saw their doubt and perplexity removed, and hope and courage animated their hearts. . . . It bore the characteristics that mark the work of God in every age.[16]

It produced everywhere the most deep searching of heart and humiliation of soul before the God of high heaven. It caused a weaning of affections from the things of this world, a healing of controversies and animosities, a confession of wrongs, a breaking down before God, and penitent, brokenhearted supplications to Him for pardon and acceptance.

Of all the great religious movements since the days of the apostles, none have been more free from human imperfection and the wiles of Satan than was that of the autumn of 1844. Even now, after the lapse of many years, all who shared in that movement and who have stood firm upon the platform of truth still feel the holy influence of that blessed work and bear witness that it was of God.[17]

The spiritual wildfire that was sparked by the Exeter camp meeting came to be known among Adventists as the "seventh-month movement," from Samuel Snow's view that the Day of Atonement, on the tenth day of the *seventh month* in the Jewish religious year, would occur, in 1844, on the twenty-second of October.

The two major characteristics of the seventh-month movement were its deep spirituality and the uncontrolled speed with which it went, completely beyond the power of any one man or group of men to lead or hold it back. Indeed, that was the characteristic of the entire Millerite movement. The final thrust of the movement, beginning in August at the Exeter camp meeting, was simply the glorious climax.

Was it of God?

So we return to our original question: Was the Millerite movement of God? By way of summary, please note the following points, which are persuasive for me:

1. **The Millerite movement was the climax to the historical method of prophetic interpretation which gave great power to the Protestant Reformation.**
2. **It came in the last days, just when the angel told Daniel that God's people would understand the 2300-day prophecy.**

3. **Miller's experience was similar to that of others whom God has called to lead a great religious movement. There was a deep searching for truth and a profound conviction to do something about it. Miller's resistance to God's call, and God's obvious answer to his prayer, while not compelling evidences in themselves, lend strong support to the conclusion that God was behind his movement.**

4. **It should be patently obvious, even to the prejudiced observer, that Miller the farmer did not invent or engineer the Advent movement. Humanistically minded people may give their psychological and sociological reasons why the movement succeeded, and there may be some truth to their conclusions. But beyond any answers that man can give lies the fact that Miller was the tiny flame that God used to light the great fire of the 1844 movement.**

I cannot answer the question of God's direction in the 1844 movement for anyone but myself. The facts that I reviewed in this chapter and the one before compel me to the conclusion that the answer to that question is an absolute Yes.

---

1. In his *Apology and Defence (sic)*, William Miller estimated that "in nearly a thousand places Advent congregations have been raised up, numbering, as near as I can estimate, some fifty thousand believers" (page 22). According to Mervyn Maxwell, chairman of the department of church history at the Andrews University Theological Seminary, some students of the Millerite movement estimate the number of Millerites at the time of the 1844 Disappointment to have been as high as 150,000. Maxwell chooses to estimate 100,000. Nobody knows for sure how many Adventists there actually were the morning of October 22, 1844.

2. Sylvester Bliss, *Memoirs of William Miller*, p. 65, italics in the original (Froom, IV:459).

3. Wm. Miller's *Apology and Defence (sic)*, p. 9 (Froom, IV:463).

4. Bliss, pp. 77-80 (Froom, IV:467).

5. Froom, IV:482, 483.

6. Miller, p. 18 (Froom, IV:483, 484).

7. Froom, IV:484.

8. *Encyclopedia Britannica*, fifteenth edition, vol. 8, p. 88-d.

9. Miller, p. 19 (not quoted in Froom).

10. Froom, IV:552.

11. *Ibid.*, p. 554.

12. *Ibid.*, p. 556.

13. *Ibid.*, p. 642.

14. See Froom, IV:643.

15. Joseph Bates, *Second Advent Way Marks and High Heaps*, p. 31 (Froom IV:816).

16. Ellen G. White, *The Great Controversy*, p. 400.

17. Bliss, in *Advent Shield and Review*, vol. 1, p. 271. (Quoted in Ellen G. White, *The Great Controversy*, p. 401.)

CHAPTER

Five

Why the Great Disappointment?

As every good Adventist knows, Jesus did *not* come on October 22, 1844.

Suppose He had. There would be no question in anyone's mind today that, Yes, God really *did* lead in the 1844 movement.

When Jesus did not come on October 22, a large majority of Miller's 100,000 adherents abandoned their faith. The whole thing, they concluded, was a sad mistake—God had nothing to do with it. And they returned either to their former churches or to no faith at all.

In the previous two chapters I responded to the question of God's involvement in the Millerite movement by taking into consideration only those events that *preceded* the Great Disappointment. I deliberately stopped short of October 22. I believe we need to evaluate the Millerite movement on its own merits, apart from the Disappointment, if we are to understand the Disappointment at all. After nearly 150 years, the Disappointment is still too traumatic an event. The sheer magnitude of tens of thousands of sincere Christians being so certain that Jesus would return on a particular day, only to be so bitterly disappointed when He did not come, tends to skew our perception of God's part in the whole affair. It's too easy to say, "God must have been off in some distant part of the universe." By itself, the Disappointment is almost certain to lead to only one conclusion: God had no part in it.

As we study the literature that came out of the Millerite movement and the Great Disappointment, we discover that to those who held firm, equally as fundamental as the question of *what* God did on October 22 was the question of whether He did anything at all. Those who maintained their faith through that tragic night refused to believe that God was asleep or off on a long journey to a distant galaxy. They believed absolutely that somehow, in some way, God *was* at work. Only with that confidence could they ask, and answer, the question of what God *did* on that day.

I believe that we, 150 years later, must approach an evaluation of 1844 the same way. For if God *did* initiate the movement, then the Disappointment had its reasons, whether we understand them or not. The movement was genuine in spite of 75,000 overnight apostasies.[1] The belief that God was involved protects our thinking from being skewed by the magnitude of the Disappointment. But we have to reach that conclusion apart from the Disappointment and bring it to the Disappointment, for the Disappointment by itself pulls too hard the other way.

The evidence presented in the earlier chapters of this book is conclusive for me. God *did* lead in the historical method of interpretation that provided great power to the Protestant Reformation. God *did* lead in the Millerite movement, which was the logical conclusion toward which the historical method of interpretation had been tending all along. Daniel 8:14 *does* point to an end-time event that was to be understood only when the end time arrived. The Millerites lived during the beginning years of the end time, and it is to be expected that they would understand the prophecies pointing to their time. These considerations, together with the unquestionable power behind their movement, persuade me that God was indeed at work.

God's power behind the movement is evidence that it was a fulfillment of prophecy, and the fact that it fulfilled prophecy is evidence that God was behind the movement. That is circular reasoning, but it's also the best way I know to say it.

Concluding that the movement itself was divinely appointed, we must now address the question, Why the Disappointment?

God planned it

Those who are familiar with the history of the Millerite movement will recall that from 1832 to 1843 Miller and his associates mistakenly preached that 1843 was the crucial year when the 2300 days would end, and that Jesus could be expected to return about that time. Apparently nobody noticed that between 1 B.C. and A.D. 1 there is no year 0. Any computation of time periods across that point, as in the Adventist view of the 2300 days, must take that fact into account. Unfortunately, the Millerites did not at first realize this. In 1842 Charles Fitch, one of the leaders of the movement, prepared a prophecy chart that was widely used as a visual aid by Millerite preachers for the next year or two. This chart was based on the prevailing view that 1843 was the correct year. Ellen White makes the following significant statement about this mistake in Fitch's chart:

I have seen that the 1843 chart was directed by the hand of the Lord, and that it should not be altered; that the figures were as He wanted them; that *His hand was over and hid a mistake in some of the figures, so that none could see it, until His hand was removed.*[2]

God Himself hid the error from His people in 1843, and He did the same with respect to the Great Disappointment on October 22, 1844. Speaking of that time Ellen White said:

God designed to prove His people. His hand covered a mistake in the reckoning of the prophetic periods. Adventists did not discover the error, nor was it discovered by the most learned of their opponents.[3]

61

I saw the disappointment of the trusting ones, as they did not see their Lord at the expected time. *It had been God's purpose to conceal the future.*[4]

It was in the Lord's order that this disappointment should come.[5]

In other words, not only was the Millerite movement itself under God's direction, but *so was the Disappointment*. At first glance this seems very strange. Is God like a cat playing with a mouse? Does He find some sort of pleasure in wrenching our emotions? The answer is obviously No. We do not serve a God like that. If God's direction of His movement led to the Disappointment, then there must have been a reason. What was it?

God's mysterious ways

God's ways often seem deeply mysterious and incomprehensible to us. Why, for example, did He allow His Son to be born under circumstances that would cast a shadow over His reputation the rest of His life? Why didn't God arrange for Jesus to be born into the home of someone who counted enough in society to at least give him a decent entry into the world? Granted that Jesus had to die as a sacrifice for sin. Did it have to be by capital punishment, death on a cross—the form of execution reserved for the worst of criminals?

Think of the hundreds, perhaps thousands, of Jews lost to the Christian cause because they could not believe in a Messiah conceived out of wedlock. Think of the huge number of Gentiles who refused to join the church in its early years because of the ridicule that was heaped upon the Christians for their "God" who was executed by crucifixion. Had I been God, I would have figured out a better way for Jesus to be born, and I would surely have figured out a better way for Him to die!

Why was God seemingly so poor at public relations?

Habakkuk asked why God used a nation worse than the Israelites to punish them.

Jonah couldn't understand why God would predict the destruction of Nineveh in forty days and then go back on His word.

The Israelites asked why God led them out of Egypt only to wander forty years in a barren desert. Many of them charged Moses with the responsibility for their escape from slavery. As far as they were concerned, God had nothing to do with it. They were ready to return to their taskmasters!

We need constantly to remind ourselves that if we want to see God at work, we should look for the unusual. This should give us pause as we think of 1844 and the Great Disappointment. It should make us less anxious to pass the snap judgment that God was a thousand light-years away. Perhaps the very strangeness of the event—the calamity that it seemed to those who passed through it—is the greatest evidence that God *was* at work. Perhaps, instead of weakening our faith, the Great Disappointment should strengthen it!

I am reminded of a story that occurred in the fourteenth century, during the Hundred Year's War. The British were fighting the French, and King Edward III ordered his son, Prince Edward, to lead a regiment of soldiers into battle while he, the king, stood by to send in additional forces as they were needed. The young prince soon felt the need of help and sent a messenger to the king. When the reinforcements did not arrive, the prince sent a second messenger with an urgent plea for immediate assistance. The king sent back a message to the prince: "I am not so inexperienced a commander as not to know when help is needed, nor so careless a father as not to send it."

The prince was perplexed when his father did not conduct the war the way he thought it should be carried out, and he was particularly distressed that his father should leave him in what seemed to him such a perilous situation.

Our Father's ways often seem perplexing to us, especially when they cause us suffering.

However, this still does not answer the question of why God would lead His people into such a false hope. I believe that there were at least two very good reasons why God allowed the Great Disappointment to happen, and, yes, why He even took the initiative to see that it happened.

God's message at that time required it

Ellen White makes a significant statement that helps us understand why God hid from the Millerites their mistaken interpretation of the event to take place at the end of the 2300 days:

> Miller and his associates fulfilled prophecy and gave a message which Inspiration had foretold should be given to the world, but which they could not have given had they fully understood the prophecies pointing out their disappointment, and presenting another message to be preached to all nations before the Lord should come.[6]

Miller and his associates "gave a message which Inspiration had foretold should be given to the world," but they could not have preached this message *had they fully understood the prophecies pointing to their Disappointment.* They would have been foolish to preach as they did had they thought it would end in bitter disappointment.

Ellen White goes on to say that Miller and his associates would not have preached as they did had they understood that there was yet "another message to be preached to all nations before the Lord should come." We, 150 years later, understand that which God could not tell the Millerites. He planned for a grand final movement on the earth, of which the Millerites were only the beginning. His plan was that His people restore to the world all of the truths lost during the period of papal supremacy. God knew that the growth and development of this movement would take many years. He wanted to initiate this final movement with a tremendous burst of power, and He used William Miller and his associates to accomplish this. Unfortunately, He could not let the Millerites know the full extent of His final movement on the earth, for had they understood the many years this movement would take, their enthusiasm would have been dampened.

The Refiner's fire

Ellen White gives yet another reason for the 1844 Disappointment—what I call "the Refiner's fire." *The Disappoint-*

ment was a test to purge out those who were uncommitted.
Said Ellen White:

> God thus [in the October 22 Disappointment] . . . has
> tested His people, has tried their faith, has proved them,
> and seen whether they would shrink, in the hour of trial,
> from the position in which He might see fit to place
> them; and whether they would relinquish this world and
> rely with implicit confidence in the word of God.[7]

> It was in the Lord's order that this disappointment
> should come, and that hearts should be revealed.[8]

> The passing of the definite time had tested and proved
> them [God's people], and very many were weighed in the
> balance and found wanting. They loudly claimed to be
> Christians, yet in almost every particular failed to follow
> Christ.[9]

It has been God's plan all along to bring to the earth a final
message to cleanse His people of sin and prepare them to meet
Him at His coming. To accomplish this He needs messengers
who are totally dedicated, consumed with a passion for their
mission. It was particularly vital that those who first established the movement be possessed of these qualities.

*I submit that one of the purposes of the Great Disappointment
was to bring a separation between those who were truly dedicated to the truth and those who were not.* God had to weed out
all those whose dedication was less than complete. Only a very
few were willing to hold on to their faith through bitter disappointment, to agonize in prayer and earnestly search the Scrip-
tures for understanding. These were the men and women God
chose to establish His final movement on the earth. The Disappointment forced out those whose Christian experience would
only have weakened the fledgling movement.

We are reminded of the story of Gideon, whom God used to
defeat the Midianites (see Judges 6, 7). God told Gideon to
send a call throughout the land of Israel for men to join his
army and defeat the enemy. The Bible says that 30,000 re-

65

sponded. However, God told Gideon that they were too many. "Send home all those who are afraid," He said.

Twenty thousand men returned to their families. Gideon must surely have wondered whether 10,000 soldiers could defeat the enemy, but God proposed yet another test: "Send the men down to the creek in the valley and separate those who reach down with their hands to scoop up the water on the run from those who get on their hands and knees to drink."

Again Gideon followed God's instruction. Three hundred men drank on the run. The rest took their time.

"I'll use the 300 to defeat the Midianites," God said. "Send the others home."

Gideon was stunned! Defeat the huge Midianite army with 300 men? Impossible!

But God knew what He was doing. At this critical time, He could not afford to have men in His army who were only partially committed to the task. He proposed a simple test that would weed out all but those totally dedicated to the work. *God divided the people according to their commitment.*

I believe that this was one of the great reasons why God allowed—indeed required—that His people pass through the Great Disappointment of October 22, 1844. In His final movement on the earth, He could use only those utterly committed to the task. It was particularly crucial that all half-hearted soldiers be weeded out. The founders of the movement had to be dedicated.

The Refiner struck His fire on October 22, 1844!

1. As mentioned in the previous chapter, nobody has any way of knowing how many Millerites there were at the time of the Disappointment, much less how many of them gave up their faith immediately. I think it is safe to say that after the Disappointment a large majority of believers abandoned their faith immediately. Seventy-five thousand is a majority of 100,000. That is the only basis for using that figure here. I suspect that the actual number was closer to 90,000 or perhaps even 95,000.

2. *Early Writings*, p. 74, italics supplied.

3. *The Story of Redemption*, pp. 362, 363.

4. *Early Writings*, p. 246, italics supplied.

5. *Selected Messages*, bk. 2, p. 108.
6. *The Great Controversy*, p. 405.
7. *The Great Controversy*, p. 406.
8. *Selected Messages*, bk. 2, p. 108.
9. *Early Writings*, p. 246.

Six

The Seventh-day Adventist Movement

A re Seventh-day Adventists God's final messengers to the earth whom He refined out of the 1844 Disappointment? That, historically, has been our self-understanding. I accept that view, and in this chapter I will explain why.

Again I will stress, however, that what I say here is not to be taken as proof of this point. Rather, it is evidence that speaks to my faith. The events I will recount do not of themselves create my faith. Rather, I bring my faith *to* the events. Because I believe that God will have a final movement on the earth, I understand these events as a fulfillment of that faith. Because I believe that God will have an end-time people, I am able to believe that my people are that people.

Faith creates interpretation, not the other way around. Skepticism, which is really a form of faith—we might say the flip side of faith—also creates interpretation, much as skeptics may wish us to believe otherwise.

In a previous chapter I mentioned that all great religious movements seem to have arisen out of a crisis of faith. Sometimes that crisis of faith is personal, as in the case of Martin

Luther, whose personal crisis and the solution he found to it sparked the Protestant reformation.

Other crises which have prompted the beginning of a great religious movement were imposed on the pioneers of the movement from the outside, and the pioneers were generally unaware, during the time immediately following the crisis, that a new religious movement was being formed. For example, the disciples were unaware, during the months (perhaps even years) immediately following Christ's death and resurrection, that they were starting a new religious movement. They thought they were merely reforming Judaism.

Similarly, as we shall see, the pioneers of the Seventh-day Adventist Church believed for several years that they had a very short work to perform, after which Jesus would come. They had no idea that God had destined them to carry out a global task.

People do not engineer the crises out of which great religious movements arise. The disciples would never, themselves, have put Christ on a cross. When He did die in this way, their hopes were crushed, yet it was from these very crushed hopes that Christianity sprang.

God seems to understand that we humans require just such crises as the disciples confronted at Calvary to initiate significant religious movements. Thus, far from viewing the Great Disappointment as an embarrassment, we ought at least to suspect God's intervention in the lives of His people. Our understanding, from prophecy, that God will call out an end-time people to restore lost truth to the world, should cause us to bring more than a little faith to our examination of the events immediately following the 1844 crisis to see if He may not indeed have been at work.

Three groups emerge

Three groups emerged from the Disappointment of October 22, 1844. The large majority quickly abandoned their faith in William Miller's movement. It is especially important to understand that these people abandoned, not only Miller's understanding of the 2300 days, but the historical method of interpretation as a valid way to understand prophecy.

A second group to emerge from the Disappointment retained their faith in the historical method of interpretation. Miller was essentially correct in his understanding of the 2300 days, they said, including his understanding that the second coming of Christ was to occur at the end of that time. The error, they affirmed, had to do with chronology: Miller got the wrong date. These people believed that Jesus would still come very soon. Many of them believed that He would come about a year later—on or about October 22, 1845. When Jesus did not come at that time, they proposed more dates and still more dates in the future. The problem was, of course, that as each date passed and Jesus did not come, more people abandoned their faith in the historical method of interpretation, till nobody believed it any more. Though it took them longer to get there, these people can be classed with those who abandoned their faith in the historical method of interpretation the day after the Disappointment.

The third group to emerge from the Disappointment also affirmed that Miller was essentially correct, but instead of seeing his error in the date, they saw it in the event to occur on October 22, 1844. They said that Daniel 8:14 predicted, not the second coming of Christ, but rather a change in Christ's ministry in the heavenly sanctuary. It was from this group that Seventh-day Adventists eventually emerged.

It should be readily apparent why Seventh-day Adventists are about the only Christian group in the world that still adheres to the historical method of prophetic interpretation. The Disappointment effactually destroyed confidence in the historical method of interpretation in the minds of most other Christians.

Let's take a closer look at these people who came through the disappointment with their faith in the historical method intact, and who eventually became Seventh-day Adventists.

Immediately after October 22, 1844

I believe that God had two important points He wanted His people to understand in the immediate aftermath of the Great

Disappointment. First, whereas He hid the error in their understanding of what was to happen on October 22, 1844, *before* that time arrived, immediately after it passed He began revealing the truth to them. Second, He did not want the Disappointment to shake their faith in His direction over their lives. Rather, He wanted them to see the Disappointment as evidence of His leading. These points are underscored by two events that occurred immediately after October 22, 1844.

Hiram Edson's "cornfield vision" explains what happened.[1] Hiram Edson was a layman and a farmer who lived near Port Gibson, New York. Some people question whether a theologically illiterate farmer should be the one to introduce a major new doctrine to the church. That argument, of course, would call into question whether a Carpenter could be the Messiah, and it would invalidate the Carpenter's choice of Peter, Andrew, James, and John—all of whom were fishermen—as His disciples. God is much more interested in the man than in his scholarly qualifications.

Edson passed through the Disappointment. He later wrote out his recollection of what happened:

> Our expectations were raised high, and thus we looked for our coming Lord until the clock tolled 12. At midnight, the day had then passed and our disappointment would become a certainty. Our fondest hopes and expectations were blasted, and such a spirit of weeping came over us as I never experienced before. It seemed that the loss of all earthly friends could have been no comparison. We wept, and wept, till the day dawn.
>
> (Then) I began to feel there might be light and help for us in our present distress. I said to some of my brethren, Let us go to the barn. We entered the granary, shut the doors about us and bowed before the Lord. We prayed earnestly for we felt our necessity. And we continued in earnest prayer until the witness of the Spirit was given that our prayer was accepted and that light should be given—our disappointment explained and made clear and satisfactory.

After breakfast I said to one of my brethren, Let us go and see, and encourage some of our brn [brethren]. We started, and while passing through a large field I was stopped about midway of the field. Heaven seemed open to my view, and I saw distinctly, and clearly, that instead of our High Priest coming out of the Most Holy of the heavenly sanctuary to come to this earth on the tenth day of the seventh month, at the end of the 2300 days, that he for the first time entered on that day the second apartment of that sanctuary; and that he had a work to perform in the Most Holy before coming to this earth.[2]

The doctrinal implication of Edson's new insight is extremely important. William Miller, in harmony with every other interpreter of prophecy up to that time, understood the sanctuary of Daniel 8:14 to be the earth, and its cleansing to be Christ's second coming. This view precipitated the Great Disappointment. If God held His hand over the error *before* the disappointment, then within a few hours *after* the disappointment, God removed His hand and began to make the meaning of this prophecy plain. That is the significance of Hiram Edson's "cornfield vision." For the first time, someone connected with the Millerite movement understood that rather than coming *out* of the Most Holy Place in heaven to cleanse the earth by fire in 1844, Christ *entered* the Most Holy Place to begin a new phase of His mediatorial ministry.

Ellen White's first vision assures of God's leading. Throughout their entire history, Seventh-day Adventists have accepted the prophetic ministry of Ellen G. White. This prophetic ministry began sometime in December 1844. Ellen and four lady friends were praying together, probably for a greater understanding of the events that had recently transpired, when Ellen received her first vision. In her own words, here is what happened:

While we were praying, the power of God came upon me as I had never felt it before. I seemed to be surrounded with light, and to be rising higher and higher

73

from the earth. I turned to look for the advent people in the world, but could not find them, when a voice said to me: "Look again, and look a little higher." At this I raised my eyes and saw a straight and narrow path, cast up high above the world. On this path the advent people were traveling toward the city. Behind them, at the beginning of the path, was a bright light which an angel told me was the midnight cry. This light shone all along the path, that their feet might not stumble. Jesus Himself went just before His people to lead them forward, and as long as they kept their eyes fixed on Him, they were safe.[3]

This vision takes up a little over three pages in volume 1 of *Testimonies for the Church*. In this beginning paragraph, God gave to Ellen White a view of His people who emerged from the 1844 Disappointment. His purpose was to help the disappointed Millerites understand that He had indeed been leading them. Ellen White went on to say:

Others [of the disappointed Millerites] rashly denied the light behind them, and said it was not God that had led them out so far. The light behind them went out, leaving their feet in perfect darkness, and they stumbled and lost sight of the mark and of Jesus, and fell off the path down into the dark and wicked world below.[4]

At the time she wrote these words, Ellen White had in mind those Millerites who totally abandoned their faith in the prophecies and returned to their former churches or to no faith at all. However, there can be no doubt that her warning applies today as well. If Ellen White was indeed God's messenger as she claimed, then we who live in the late 1900s need to be just as careful how we treat the events surrounding the Millerite movement and the Great Disappointment as did those who passed through that time. It is just as dangerous to deny the meaning of those events now as it was then.

To turn the question around, *it is just as important for us to recognize God's hand in the Millerite movement, the Great Dis-appointment, and the events immediately thereafter, as it was for those who experienced them.* Our faith is as much tied to what happened then as was theirs. The tragedy is that the majority of Adventists in the late 1900s are only vaguely aware of what happened in the 1840s, and a significant number of those who do know what happened deny the importance of those events.

From 1845 to 1850

In just two or three years after 1844, our early pioneers hammered out the basic doctrinal positions that we still hold as a body. One can argue that these humble people, untrained in the skills of theology, are a poor foundation on which to base a worldwide mission to finish God's work in the earth; or one can argue that the very fact that untrained minds were able to establish the solid positions we still hold 150 years later is evidence that God was with them. Because so many of our people are unaware of the early development of our teachings, I will briefly review that history here.

The Sabbath. A Seventh Day Baptist woman named Rachel Oaks Preston introduced the Sabbath to Frederick Wheeler, a Methodist clergyman who became the first Adventist minister to preach in favor of the Sabbath. However, the Sabbath truth came more directly to the pioneers of the Seventh-day Adventist Church through Joseph Bates. Bates learned about the Sabbath in February 1845, from an article by T. M. Preble that was published in a Millerite paper, *The Hope of Israel.* After checking the biblical evidence for himself, Bates became convinced that it taught the truth and immediately began keeping the day. The following year he wrote a forty-eight-page tract, *The Seventh-day Sabbath, a Perpetual Sign,* in which he pointed out that the papacy had changed the day from the seventh to the first day of the week, thus fulfilling the prophecy of Daniel 7:25. In a revised edition of his tract published the following year he made a special point of the Sabbath as a part of the third angel's message, referring to the observance of Sunday as a mark of the beast.

James and Ellen White learned of the Sabbath from Joseph Bates shortly after their marriage on August 30, 1846. At first they resisted this teaching, but further study convinced them that it was scriptural, and sometime during the fall of the year they began to keep it. From that day till the day of her death, Ellen White was an ardent advocate of the Sabbath. She fully adopted the view, first suggested by Bates and later elaborated by others, that the Sabbath was the seal of God, and Sunday observance, when enforced by law, the mark of the beast.

The state of the dead. Another pillar of Seventh-day Adventist teaching is that of man's unconsciousness in death. George Storrs, a Methodist minister, began to advance this view even before the Disappointment of 1844. He also taught that God will not punish the wicked with everlasting torment. In fact, so influential was Storrs in this regard that four of the five religious bodies that exist today as remnants of the Millerite movement still teach that the soul is unconscious after death.

Christ's ministry in the sanctuary. We have already noted that the morning after the Great Disappointment, Hiram Edson received an insight into Christ's change of ministry in the heavenly sanctuary. However, this was only a hint—a suggestion from God that would require intense study to develop into a complete doctrine.

In his account of events the morning after October 22, Hiram Edson mentions inviting a brother who was a guest in his home to accompany him on a visit to some of the other brethren. Edson does not tell us who this brother was, but another Adventist pioneer, J. N. Loughborough, informs us that it was a man by the name of O. R. L. Crosier.[5] Edson and Crosier went to the home of F. B. Hahn, a Millerite who was also a physician. The three of them spent the next year in an intensive study of Edson's new insights. A year later Crosier wrote a long article, with extensive scriptural documentation, that explained Edson's "cornfield vision" in minute detail. This article appeared twice, the second time in its most complete form in *The Day Star* Extra, February 7, 1846. Ellen White was extremely impressed with Crosier's work, placing it on her recommended reading list:

> I believe the Sanctuary, to be cleansed at the end of the 2300 days, is the New Jerusalem Temple, of which Christ is a minister. The Lord shew [sic] me in vision, more than one year ago, that Brother Crosier had the true light on the cleansing of the Sanctuary, &c; and that it was his will, that Brother C. should write out the view which he gave us in the Day-Star Extra, February 7, 1846. I feel fully authorized by the Lord to recommend that Extra, to every saint.[6]

The major doctrines that Seventh-day Adventists still teach were developed by just a handful of people between 1845 and 1847.[7] Ellen White says that often they would spend entire nights on their knees, with their Bibles in front of them, pleading with God for an understanding of truth. Sometimes, after they had reached a conclusion, God would confirm it through a vision given to Ellen White. At other times when, after hours of study a particular point still puzzled them, she would receive a vision that suggested the direction their study should take. Prophetic confirmation gave this handful of believers complete confidence in the validity of their new understanding of truth—a confidence they would have to have in order to carry it to the world.

Carrying the truth to other Millerites. Thus, by the end of 1847, two or three dozen people had developed the basic teachings that Adventists hold to the present time. Now another important task faced them: uniting other Millerite believers around these teachings. This was accomplished largely through six meetings that have come to be known as "Sabbath conferences." According to James White, who wrote of them several years later, the purpose of these conferences was "uniting the brethren on the great truths connected with the message of the third angel."[8]

The first of these conferences was held at Rocky Hill, Connecticut, in April 1848. James White described the meeting in a letter:

We arrived at this place about four P.M. In a few minutes in came Brn. Bates and Gurney. We had a meeting that evening of about fifteen in all. Friday morning the brethren came in until we numbered about fifty. They were not all fully in the truth. Our meeting that day was very interesting. Bro. Bates presented the commandments in a clear light, and their importance was urged home by powerful testimonies. The word had effect to establish those already in the truth, and to awaken those who were not fully decided.[9]

Five similar conferences were held throughout New England during 1848. Six more conferences were held during 1849, and ten in 1850. James and Ellen White attended all of the conferences in 1848, and most of those in 1849 and 1850.

Adventist growth since 1850

In 1847 there were probably not 100 people in all the world who accepted the teachings that we have believed for nearly 150 years. Had I lived back then, it would have stretched my imagination to the breaking point to suppose that God had in mind for these few people to establish a worldwide movement for the finishing of His work. Was this tiny band really destined by God to carry His final warning message to the world? Is there evidence since 1850 that God directed in the establishment of our church through these few Millerites, giving them the divine commission found in the three angels' messages as we have historically taught?

As our final step in answering this question, I would like for you to review with me just briefly the growth of our church since 1850. We will also examine the contribution Ellen White made to this growth.

Growth since 1850. Of the religious bodies which sprang from the 1844 Disappointment, only four continue to the present time,[10] some with memberships of only a few hundred. The Advent Christian Church, a Sunday-keeping group with less than 20,000 members in America today, has almost no work outside the United States. By contrast, Seventh-day Adventists have a worldwide membership that, as of this writing, is moving rapidly toward 6 million adherents.

Though Seventh-day Adventists are still one of the smaller Christian denominations, since 1850 we have established one of the largest Protestant mission programs in the world. Our church currently operates the largest Protestant health-care system in the world as well as the largest nonprofit health-care organization in the United States. We operate the largest Protestant educational system in the world and one of the largest in the United States, and worldwide we operate the largest Protestant publishing program.

If God had in mind to establish a worldwide movement out of the 1844 disappointment, I have no difficulty choosing the right one from among the five available candidates! Which one has come the closest to getting the job done?

Ministry of Ellen G. White. Ellen White has never been popular outside the Adventist Church, and even in some Adventist circles she has become rather unpopular of late. However, I believe even her critics would agree that the outstanding achievements of this church are to a great degree attributable to her vision and encouragement. Because the church's leadership believed that she spoke for God, they generally followed her advice. Who can argue with the results?

To my mind, one of the strongest evidences that Ellen White was God's messenger is the phenomenal achievement of her life. Her ministry is one of the strongest evidences that Seventh-day Adventists are who they claim to be—God's end-time people, with the mission of finishing His work on the earth.

Also, Ellen White's understanding of last-day events is extremely relevant today. Notice the following points:

1. **Based on the historical interpretation of prophecy, she predicted that Catholicism would revive from its deadly wound to a position of worldwide respect and prominence. This view must have seemed quite odd to people during the late nineteenth century, when anti-Catholicism was run-**

ning so rampant in America, but *Ellen White's prediction has now been fulfilled.*

2. **She predicted that spiritualism would become a popular movement of worldwide proportions just before the end of time. The New Age movement provides ample evidence that *this prediction has now been fulfilled.***

3. **She predicted that Protestants would abandon their historic position regarding church and state and would appeal to the state to intervene on behalf of public morality. *That prediction is now clearly in the process of being fulfilled.***

The emergence of the Seventh-day Adventist Church from the 1844 crisis, the outstanding growth of our movement, together with the impressive fulfillment in recent years of Ellen White's predictions regarding last-day events, leave me more persuaded than ever that this church *was* raised up by God, and that we *do* have an extremely significant role to play in preparing the world to face the critical issues that lie just ahead.

---

1. Hiram Edson does not say that his new insight into Christ's ministry in the heavenly sanctuary occurred in a cornfield. That bit of information comes from J. N. Loughborough, who was not present at the time but undoubtedly heard it from Edson (see J. N. Loughborough, *The Great Second Advent Movement*, p. 193). Also, Edson does not call his experience in the cornfield a "vision," as some have taught. He says, "I saw," which could mean a vision but does not have to. The *SDA Encyclopedia*, revised edition, says that "an overwhelming conviction came over him" (page 413).

2. Fragment of a letter written by Hiram Edson.

3. *Testimonies for the Church*, vol. 1, pp. 58, 59.

4. *Ibid.*, p. 59.

5. J. N. Loughborough, *The Great Second Advent Movement: Its Rise and Progress* (Review and Herald Publishing Association: Battle Creek, Mich., 1905, 1909), p. 193.

6. Letter to Eli Curtis, written at Topsham, Maine, April 21, 1847, emphasis supplied.

7. During most of our history Adventist historians have thought

that the early development of our teachings occurred during the 1848 Sabbath conferences. However, a more recent view is that this doctrinal development took place prior to 1848, the task from 1848 onward being to unite others around truths already established.

8. *Review and Herald*, May 6, 1852, quoted in the *Seventh-day Adventist Encyclopedia*, revised edition, p. 1255.

9. *Spiritual Gifts*, vol. 2, p. 93.

10. Advent Christian Church (no membership statistics given, but their headquarters in Charlotte, North Carolina informed me in a telephone call that their membership in the United States and Canada at the end of 1987 was 19,261); Church of God General Conference (Oregon, Ill.), 5,759 members; Primitive Advent Christian Church, 546 members; Seventh-day Adventists (in the United States, 1985), 623,623 according to the *1985 Yearbook of American and Canadian Churches*, published by the National Council of Churches. Not listed under "Adventist Bodies" are two groups: the Church of God (7th Day), Salem, West Virginia (in a telephone conversation I was told that this group does not keep membership statistics); and Church of God (Seventh Day), Denver, Colorado, 5,249 members. These two Sabbath-keeping denominations are not direct descendents of the Millerite movement, but are successors of the now defunct Church of God Adventist, an early splinter group from Seventh-day Adventists (see the *Seventh-day Adventist Encyclopedia* revised edition, "Marion Party," pp. 853, 854).

Seven

Purpose of the Advent Movement

W e have come to the point in our study where we must ask, If Seventh-day Adventists indeed have a special work to do for God in the last days of earth's history, what is it? What does God expect of His people in preparation for the end time? What does He expect of *me*? Can I meet His expectations? Once we recognize that an understanding of the Seventh-day Adventist message places us under a special obligation, it is imperative that we understand clearly what that obligation is and how we can successfully carry it out.

In this chapter I will discuss what I understand our mission to be from two perspectives, both suggested by Ellen White. These two concepts may seem to be unrelated at first, but they are, in fact, bound very closely together. One has to do with preparing to live without a Mediator, and the other is Ellen White's "John the Baptist" view of the remnant church.

Preparing to live without a Mediator

In her book *The Great Controversy*, Ellen White discusses very specifically the preparation God's people must make in order to be ready for the end time. Speaking of God's people immediately after the 1844 Disappointment, she makes a rather long and significant statement, which we will consider in short sections. In the first two sentences of this extended statement, she gives one of the most important reasons why Jesus did *not* return in 1844:

The people were not yet ready to meet their Lord. There was still a work of preparation to be accomplished for them.[1]

What is this work that must still be accomplished for God's people in order to prepare them for Christ's return? Ellen White answered that question by quoting Malachi 3:2, 3:

Says the prophet: "Who may abide the day of His coming? and who shall stand when He appeareth? for he is like a refiner's fire, and like fullers' soap: and He shall sit as a refiner and purifier of silver: and He shall purify the sons of Levi, and purge them as gold and silver, that they may offer unto the Lord an offering in righteousness."

And now comes what many find to be one of Ellen White's most fearful statements. Without question, it is one of her most misunderstood. Much of the next three chapters will be devoted to understanding the ideas expressed here and in one or two statements similar to this one. She says:

Those who are living upon the earth when the intercession of Christ shall cease in the sanctuary above are to stand in the sight of a holy God without a mediator. Their robes must be spotless, their characters must be purified from sin by the blood of sprinkling. Through the grace of God and their own diligent effort they must be conquerors in the battle with evil. While the investigative judgment is going forward in heaven, while the sins of penitent believers are being removed from the sanctuary, there is to be a special work of purification, of putting away of sin, among God's people upon earth.

This is a startling idea, but please notice what follows immediately after, in the next paragraph:

When this work shall have been accomplished, the followers of Christ will be ready for His appearing.

In the opening sentence of the extended passage that we have been considering from *The Great Controversy*, Ellen White says that one of the reasons Jesus did not return in 1844 is that God's people were *not* ready to meet Him. Those who came through the Disappointment with their faith intact were actually very highly committed Christians. They had to be, or they would have abandoned their faith as so many others did at that time. *But they were not ready for Christ's return.* According to Ellen White, God's people must engage in a very special spiritual preparation in order to pass through the very last days of this earth's history. The reason for such a special preparation is that a situation will prevail just before Christ returns that has never existed on earth or in heaven before: For the first time since the fall of man, probation will have closed, and there will be no Mediator in the heavenly sanctuary.

This unique theological view has produced two unfortunate results.

First, the suggestion that we must be perfect—"[our] robes must be spotless, [our] characters must be purified from sin by the blood of sprinkling" in order to live without a Mediator—this thought has driven some Seventh-day Adventists to the point of despair. "I can never be that good," they declare, and they give up. Others put forth noble efforts to "be good," but they are constantly frustrated by the sin that they continue to see in themselves. The most frightening thought of all, of course, is that "Jesus might close the door of probation before I'm ready!"

For more than a hundred years Adventists have been faced with a contradiction. We perceive ourselves as God's special people for this time in history, with the significant mission of preparing the world for the close of probation, the time of trouble, and Christ's return; yet that very mission causes us great fear and uncertainty.

Second, this issue has fueled a great deal of theological controversy since 1888. The conflict is particularly sharp on two related points: righteousness by faith and the nature of Christ. I will discuss these difficult questions in two subsequent chapters. My purpose here is simply to point out that our mission to prepare the world for the end time has produced an unusual and unncesessary amount of fear and theological controversy which have clouded our view of the mission itself.

Adventists preparing for the end time need hope!

We need hope, first of all, that we can make it through, and we need hope that the controversy over our mission and its theological implications won't tear us apart.

I want to assure you that we can have that hope.

John the Baptist and the remnant church

Matthew and Luke both assured their readers that John the Baptist's mission fulfilled Isaiah's prediction that just before the coming of the Messiah a prophet would arise proclaiming, "In the desert prepare the way for the Lord; make straight in the wilderness a highway for our God" (Isaiah 40:3, NIV; see also Matthew 3:1-3, Luke 3:1-6).

Repeatedly throughout her writings, Ellen White says that just as God raised up John the Baptist to prepare the way for Christ's first coming, so He raised up the Seventh-day Adventist Church to prepare the way for His second coming. As Ellen White understood it, John's message is ours:

What is our work? The same as that given to John the Baptist, of whom we read: "In those days came John the Baptist, preaching in the wilderness of Judea, and saying, Repent ye: for the kingdom of heaven is at hand."[2]

Our message must be as direct as was that of John. . . . Our work in this age must be as faithfully done. . . . With the earnestness that characterized Elijah the prophet and John the Baptist, we are to strive to prepare the way for Christ's second advent.[3]

According to Matthew, John preached repentance for sin as a necessary preparation for the kingdom of God. Repentance means understanding the issues of life, especially our attitudes, the way God does. It means judging our motives the way God does, sorting right from wrong within our thoughts and feelings. However, it is not enough to recognize sin in our life. When we recognize a difference between God's pattern and our way of life, we should want to be like the pattern, and that desire should translate into specific actions in an effort to change.

Does repentance also include sorrow for sin? Yes, but repentance can also manifest itself as great joy, as in the case of the man who found a treasure chest in the field. Some people have felt frustrated with their way of life and have been searching for God's way of life for a long time. When they find it, they feel ecstatic.

This truth about repentance was underscored for me several years ago when I was pastoring a church in Texas. I had always taught the people to whom I gave Bible studies that coming to Jesus meant feeling sorrow for sin. One day I asked a young lady who had recently joined the church whether she felt this way when she first learned the truth. "Oh, no!" she said. "I felt great joy."

Her response caused me to realize that I had been imposing a single response to Jesus on my students. That which *some* people experience I expected of *everyone*. Please don't misunderstand. I believe that from time to time every Christian will experience repentance as sorrow. But in every Christian's life there will also be great joy at discovering certain truths—even difficult truths about his or her own personal life.

As I have defined it here, repentance should be a way of life. That's a gloomy thought if by repentance we mean sorrow. But if repentance means recognizing God's way of life and desiring to make it one's own, and if this experience often brings great joy, then repentance ought to be a way of life.

Please notice that John the Baptist did not merely call people to repent. He said, "Repent, *for the kingdom of heaven is near*" (Matthew 3:2, NIV). The reason for the urgency of John's message was that God was about to come in human form. His people would have the marvelous opportunity of touching Him, seeing Him, and hearing Him talk to them face to face. But it would be impossible for men and women to experience God in this new, intimate way without repentance as a way of life, for Jesus would come teaching God's way of life, and only those who wanted God's way of life for themselves could benefit from His presence. Furthermore, there would be only three and a half years for God's people to experience this close personal relationship with Jesus. No wonder John's message was so urgent!

We live at a time when God's people will see God and Jesus Christ face to face, in their full glory. We will be changed from mortality to immortality. We will be ushered into heaven itself, and into the fellowship of all the holy beings throughout the universe. But only those who understand the issues of life the way God does today will be allowed to experience the presence of God, heaven, and the angels tomorrow. That is why John the Baptist's message of repentance is ours. That is why Ellen White compares our work so closely to his.

As Adventists understand Christian history, for nearly 2,000 years Satan worked within the church itself to distort the truth about God. Millions of Christians have come to believe that blatant error is orthodox truth. It is God's purpose in these last days to restore fully His truth to the world in preparation for the time of trouble and Christ's return. He wants us to restore the truth about His character as revealed in the Sabbath, the plan of salvation, the sanctuary message, and His plan for the eternal destiny of both the righteous and the wicked. Understanding these truths is essential if we are successfully to endure the time of trouble. God's people who still cling to error must repent. Some will experience this repentance as sorrow, but we should all experience it as joy.

If Ellen White says anything at all about preparing for the times just ahead, she informs us that those who pass through the close of probation and the time of trouble successfully must experience a closeness to Christ, and through that closeness a transformation of character of the highest degree. This is necessary because during that time there will be no Mediator in the heavenly sanctuary. Some Adventists may wish she *didn't* mean that, and some may even argue that she *shouldn't* mean that, but I believe few will argue that she *doesn't* mean that. As you continue reading this book, you will discover that repentance lies at the very foundation of the preparation God wants you and me to make for the time when there will be no Mediator in the heavenly sanctuary.

The nature of that preparation will be the subject of the next few chapters.

---

1. *The Great Controversy*, pp. 424, 425, emphasis supplied.

2. *Testimonies for the Church*, vol. 8, p. 9.

3. Ellen G. White Comments, *Seventh-day Adventist Bible Commentary*, vol. 4, p. 1184.

SECTION
Two

Preparing for the End Time

Eight

The Close of Probation

W hen I was a freshman at Southwestern Junior College (now Southwestern Adventist College) in Keene, Texas, the Bible teacher required each student to prepare a chart of last-day events, with full documentation from the Bible and the writings of Ellen White.

Back then, college students in Keene, Texas, were not the only ones engaged in this remarkable exercise. Preparing last-day-events charts used to be a favorite Adventist pastime. It's not so much anymore. Maybe it ought to be. In spite of the fact that these charts tended to be somewhat speculative, and some people went overboard in their fascination with lining up the order of last-day events, I believe the charts themselves were beneficial. They kept Adventists aware of their unique place in the final days of earth's history. They reminded us of our mission. Anything that does that in a reasonably balanced way is, to my way of thinking, healthy.

The basic concepts of Adventist eschatology that I learned in that class have stayed with me to the present time. My understanding has expanded a great deal, to be sure, but the outline is still the same.

There are two key events, yet future, about which we may be absolutely certain from the information given us in the Bible and the writings of Ellen White. One is the close of probation. The other is the second coming of Christ a short time later. In this chapter we will focus our attention on the close of probation and the events that lead up to it.

What is the close of probation?

In modern legal terminology, probation is a period of grace that a judge imposes in lieu of a jail term on a person who is guilty of a crime. The criminal's probation is normally fixed at a predetermined length of time, during which he must report regularly to an officer of the law and stay out of further trouble.

Probation in the religious sense has somewhat the same meaning, but there are significant differences.

When Adam and Eve sinned, they changed their allegiance from God to Satan. Satan now claimed them as citizens of his kingdom, subject to his dominion. However, Christ paid the penalty for man's sin, and man now has the opportunity of changing his allegiance back to God.

The time granted to people during which they can change their allegiance back to God is what Christians, and especially Adventists, mean when they speak of "human probation."

However, *man's opportunity to choose which master he will serve must eventually come to an end*. If the opportunity to choose whom we will serve is probation, then the conclusion of that opportunity is the close of probation.

Probation in modern legal terms applies to a period of a few years in the life of a criminal. However, in the Christian sense, probationary time extends over most of world history. The world's probation is so long that most people were born and have died within that time. At any time during their lives, they have had the opportunity of changing their allegiance from Satan back to God. Conversely, those who are on God's side can change their allegiance back to Satan anytime they so choose. However, if a time is coming when probation will close, then obviously the people born just before that time will be alive when probation closes. These people will only have the opportunity to change their allegiance from Satan to God (or vice versa) before probation's close, not after.

We have already discussed at some length Ellen White's view that when Christ ceases His mediatorial ministry in the heavenly sanctuary, earth's inhabitants, including God's own people, must "stand in the sight of a holy God without a mediator."[1] The conclusion of Christ's mediatorial ministry in the heavenly sanctuary is the close of probation.

We are now ready to consider some of the implications of the idea that probationary time will close someday, and that that day is very near.

Only two classes of people

It seems logical to assume that when probation closes there will be only two classes of people: those who have chosen to be on God's side and those who have chosen to remain with Satan. Scripture sometimes associates this division with Christ's second coming, as in the parable of the sheep and the goats:

> When the Son of Man comes in his glory, and all the angels with him, he will sit on his throne in heavenly glory. All the nations will be gathered before him, and he will separate the people one from another as a shepherd separates the sheep from the goats. He will put the sheep on his right and the goats on his left (Matthew 25:31-33, NIV).

Revelation 13 and 14 describe these same two classes of people, only here they are distinguished by a mark for the wicked and a seal for the righteous.

At the present time there are three classes of people in the world, the third class being those who have not yet finalized their choice. But how can this class of people ever be significantly diminished, to say nothing of eliminated altogether? Thousands of babies are born each day. This constantly resupplies the class of people who have not yet had an opportunity to make a choice for God or Satan. How can God close probation when there are always new people coming along to resupply that third class?

According to Revelation 13 and 14, the events that transpire in the world just before the end of time will force every human being to make a decision for or against God. At that time God and Satan will each put forth a total effort to convert people to their side. God will pour out His Spirit in latter-rain power, and in response, Satan will bring intense persecution to bear on those loyal to God (see Revelation 18:1; 13:15).

Seventh-day Adventists understand that the great issue in the final conflict will be over the Sabbath of the fourth commandment. We expect that strict Sunday laws will be enacted, first in the United States and eventually around the world, severely restricting the freedom of God's people to worship as they choose and eventually condemning all Sabbath keepers to death. This pressure will force everyone to make a decision for or against God. At that time it will be impossible for any thinking adult to remain uncommitted.

If we believe that probation's close is near, and that it is very likely to occur within the lifetime of human beings who live on the earth today, the next logical question—one that almost jumps up and down demanding an answer—is, *When* will probation close?

Adventists teach that the close of probation will occur a short time before the second coming of Christ. This idea is suggested in the Bible (see Revelation 15, 16), and it is plainly stated in the writings of Ellen White:

When the work of the investigative judgment closes, the destiny of all will have been decided for life or death. *Probation is ended a short time before the appearing of the Lord in the clouds of heaven. . . .*

The righteous and the wicked will still be living upon the earth in their mortal state—men will be planting and building, eating and drinking, all unconscious that the final, irrevocable decision has been pronounced in the sanctuary above.[2]

Whereas Christ's second coming will be earthshaking—an event that can escape no one's attention—the close of probation will be silent, invisible, imperceptible. People will not realize their danger. Even Adventists today are largely unaware of the seriousness of the time.

Life goes on so easily!

The judgment of the living

The close of probation can be thought of in two ways: individual and corporate. If by "the close of probation" we mean the time when the eternal destiny of individuals is fixed beyond change, then in a very real sense probation has been closing ever since the beginning of time, for each individual's probation closes at the time he dies. However, when Adventists speak of the close of probation, they have in mind corporate probation, that is, probation for the human race as a whole.

As Adventists understand it, the pre-advent judgment began in 1844 with a review of the lives of those who first died on the earth. Abel's name was presumably the first to come up. Long ago, God and the angels must have finished judging those who died before 1844. We can speculate that sometime during the latter half of the nineteenth century, the judgment passed from those who died in the past to those dying in the present. Since that time, the judgment has merely been a "catch-up" affair—judging people as they die.

However, if probation is to close for all human beings before Christ comes, then at some point God and the angels must begin passing final judgment not only upon people *as* they die, but *before* they die. Ellen White refers to this as "the judgment of the living."[3] In the late 1800's she wrote:

> The judgment has been over forty years in progress on the cases of the dead, and we know not how soon it will pass to the cases of the living.[4]

It would perhaps be most accurate to think of the corporate

97

close of probation as a series of events in the lives of many individuals, all of which add up to the close of probation for the entire world. This process begins with the judgment of the living and ends when Christ ceases His mediatorial ministry above. During this time it will still be possible for people on earth to make a final decision for or against God, because Jesus' mediatorial ministry will still be in progress. When every human being alive on the earth has made a final decision for or against God, the probation of every human being on earth will have closed. When that time comes, Jesus' mediatorial ministry in heaven will also close, because there will be no one left for His ministry to benefit. Understood in this way, the close of probation is not an arbitrary decision on God's part to ring down the curtain. The close of probation is really a human decision. It is the combined decisions of all human beings. And it is God's recognition of that combined decision.

The idea that the close of probation will be an arbitrary decision on God's part has created a great deal of fear among some Adventists. This fear is illustrated by something an Adventist woman told me one day. "I'm terribly afraid," she said, "that probation might close and I won't be ready." It's as though God were to say, "John, Mary, I really think a lot of you. You're converted, and I know you love Me. I surely wish there were just a couple more years, because I know you'd be ready by then. Unfortunately, the time has come for the close of probation. I'm so sorry."

Understand that God will not close probation while there is even one person who might turn to Christ. God will not close probation while one of His children is in the process of spiritual growth, but is not quite ready to receive the seal of God. *If you love Jesus with all your heart and want nothing more than to spend eternity with Him, then do not fear that probation might close before you are ready.*

The rapture theory and the close of probation

Satan nearly always invents a false theory to match the important truths of God's Word. The close of probation is such a crucial event that we should hardly be surprised to find that he has invented an alternative to that as well. It is called the "secret rapture." Here is a diagram that compares the rapture view with the Adventist view:

The Rapture	**The Rapture View**	The Second Coming
	The Tribulation	

The Close of Probation	**The Adventist View**	The Second Coming
	The Time of Trouble	

According to the rapture theory, all Christians alive at the time of the rapture will be taken to heaven, where they will spend the seven years of the tribulation. In other words, Christians will be spared the trials of the tribulation, or time of trouble. The rapture theory also teaches that huge numbers of Jews will be converted during the tribulation, and that any Gentile who was not a Christian at the time of the rapture will have another chance at salvation. Furthermore, *any Christian who was not quite ready for the rapture will also have a second chance during the tribulation to prepare for the second coming of Christ.* Millions of conservative, Bible-believing Christians have accepted this false teaching.

The close similarity between the Adventist view and the rapture view suggests that the rapture is a counterfeit of Satan, designed to lull God's people into the false security that they will have a second chance after the rapture. This is Satan's false substitute for God's warning about the close of probation, following which there will be no second chance.

The close of probation and our mission

The close of probation has everything to do with the mission of the Seventh-day Adventist Church. I think it should be

99

plain to every reader by now that the really critical time in the events before us is not so much the second coming of Christ as it is the close of probation. The close of probation will come silently, and nobody will know when it has happened. Yet this is the process, and the event, by which human destiny is forever fixed beyond the possibility of change.

God has told Seventh-day Adventists about this critical time that lies just ahead. We understand the issues in the great conflict that is soon to break upon the world. We know that the Sabbath is to be the great issue that divides the human race into two camps. We know that spiritualism is Satan's masterpiece of deception to deceive God's people in the last days. We understand the difference between the close of probation and Satan's false substitute, the rapture theory. Seventh-day Adventists understand these things, *but nobody else does.*

No other Christian church on the face of the earth teaches these truths that are so critical for our time. God has millions of people in these churches, and millions of others who belong to no church, whom He wants us to warn. We are His "John the Baptists" in these last days to prepare the world for His coming. We may relax and take our ease, as so many of us are doing at the present time, but *God holds us responsible*. If we believe at all in the Seventh-day Adventist message, and if we believe at all in the messages God has given us through Ellen White, *then we must act upon what we know!*

Unfortunately, there is not a lot of time left in which to act!

If you are among those who have been afraid of the close of probation, fearful that you might not be ready, I hope that what you learned in this chapter dispels that fear. Because you cannot act your part in these last days the way God wants you to as long as that fear remains in your heart. It is my earnest desire that what you read in this chapter, and what you will read in the rest of this book, will give you hope and also a new vision for who you are as a Seventh-day Adventist, and that you will be moved to take a more active part in the real mission of your church.

1. *The Great Controversy*, p. 425.

2. *The Great Controversy*, pp. 490, 491, emphasis supplied.

3. In a sense we might say that the judgment of the living has been going on since the beginning of time. Some people, such as Enoch and Elijah among the righteous, and Saul and Judas among the wicked, probably closed their probation a short time before their translation or death, and from time to time perhaps others among both the righteous and the wicked have done the same. But what was a trickle throughout most of world history will become a flood as massive numbers of human beings are forced to make their final decisions because of the intense pressure of last-day events.

4. *Testimonies for the Church*, vol. 5, p. 692.

Nine

How Perfect Must I Be?

We are now ready to consider some issues that have troubled Seventh-day Adventists for decades. Many of us fear that perhaps we are not quite "good enough" to make it safely through the end time. The effort of some to make themselves good enough has led to endless debate over righteousness by faith and the nature of Christ.

Adventist editors—of whom I happen to be one—are all too familiar with the intensity of feeling that these discussions can arouse. All we have to do is publish a magazine article or a book that appears to be sympathetic to the views of one side in these controversies, and soon the angry letters and telephone calls start to pour in from the other side, accusing us, our journals, and our publishing houses of printing heresy. I almost hesitate to raise these issues in this book, because I know, inevitably, what the reaction may be.

However, I also believe the fear generated through our misunderstanding of these issues, and the bitter conflict that has resulted from our debating of them, has too long kept us from going through to the second coming of Christ. I am persuaded that there is no need for us to be afraid of whether we are "good enough." Somehow, we must find answers that will give us assurance and on which we can all agree enough that the spirit of contention disappears.

Before we get into a discussion of these issues, I would like to bring to your attention a statement that Ellen White made many years ago:

> Those who cannot impartially examine the evidences of a position that differs from theirs, are not fit to teach in any department of God's cause.[1]

I'm sure Ellen White had a good reason for saying that the way she did. She was, no doubt, writing to someone who needed those negative words. I'm concerned, though, that there is already too much negative thinking over these matters within our church. If there is one thing above another I want to avoid in this book, it is any suggestion that I feel critical or hostile toward those who disagree with my views. I think it would better suit our purposes here if we turned that negative statement into a positive one, like this:

> The ones best equipped to teach in any department of God's cause are those who can impartially examine the evidences of a position that differs from theirs.

I also like what Ellen White says in the next couple of paragraphs. Here she speaks more positively, and she reflects the spirit that I believe all of us need as we approach these difficult questions:

> When the Spirit of God rests upon you, there will be no feeling of envy or jealousy in examining another's position; there will be no spirit of accusation and criticism, such as Satan inspired in the hearts of the Jewish leaders against Christ. . . . *We should come into a position where every difference will be melted away.*[2]

I hope you do not think I mean that we should all come into full agreement on every point. That would be impossible, and unhealthy if it could be made to happen. I welcome the opportunity of investigating the views of those who differ with me, because I have found that my own thinking expands and grows best when I have the opportunity of interacting with a variety of ideas. I recognize that some views are right and others wrong, and we make decisions about which is which. It is the *spirit* of our discussions that concerns me here, not their content. No decision is right, be it ever so theologically correct, that is made in a wrong spirit.

Some of the concepts most valuable to me in resolving theological difficulties have come through interaction with people whose views were vastly different from mine and with whom I could never agree. I would have missed these opportunities for growth had I come at their ideas with my fangs bared. It is not differences of opinion that trouble me, but the spirit of criticism over those differences.

Even if you disagree with me, I hope that what I say in the next few chapters will stimulate your mind to think in new ways and that as a result you will understand more clearly. If that happens, please write and tell me what you've learned, because I'm sure that your fresh ideas will help me understand better too—even if I disagree with you!

One more point: Please do not think I am trying to offer the last word on these issues that have become so controversial among Seventh-day Adventists. My primary purpose is to relate these questions to the end time in such a way that Adventists awaiting the close of probation and the time of trouble can have hope, not fear. I believe that discussion of the problems and unresolved questions is important, and ought to continue—albeit in a greater spirit of harmony. At the same time, we should continue preparing for what lies ahead, recognizing that we don't have to solve every single theological difficulty in order to be adequately prepared to go through the time of trouble.

With this preface, let us get into our subject.

The basis of the problem

The root of the problem lies in a statement by Ellen White that we quoted several chapters back:

Those who are living upon the earth when the intercession of Christ shall cease in the sanctuary above are to stand in the sight of a holy God without a mediator. Their robes must be spotless, their characters must be purified from sin by the blood of sprinkling. Through the grace of God and their own diligent effort they must be conquerors in the battle with evil. While the investigative judgment is going forward in heaven, while the sins of penitent believers are being removed from the sanctuary, there is to be a special work of purification, of putting away of sin, among God's people upon earth.[3]

We read that and we say, "Wow, I could never be that good!" I suspect that a great many Adventists have either become lukewarm, or have given up the faith altogether, because they simply could not imagine themselves reaching the "point of perfection" demanded by that statement.

Here is another well-known statement similar to the one above:

Now, while our great High Priest is making the atonement for us, we should seek to become perfect in Christ. Not even by a thought could our Saviour be brought to yield to the power of temptation. Satan finds in human hearts some point where he can gain a foothold; some sinful desire is cherished, by means of which his temptations assert their power. But Christ declared of Himself: "The prince of this world cometh, and hath nothing in Me." John 14:30. Satan could find nothing in the Son of God that would enable him to gain the victory. He had kept His Father's commandments, and there was no sin in Him that Satan could use to his advantage. *This is the condition in which those must be found who shall stand in the time of trouble.*[4]

Perhaps this is a good place to deviate a moment and point out that there are two ways to think of perfection. In one sense, we are perfect in Jesus the moment we accept Him as our Saviour, because His righteousness covers our sins. On the other hand, character perfection continues during one's entire lifetime. Just as a baby is perfect as a baby, but not as a mature adult, so we can be perfect at the beginning of our Christian walk while still looking forward to continual growth as we mature in the Christian life. Ellen White refers to both aspects of perfection in the following statement:

At every stage of development our life may be perfect; yet if God's purpose for us is fulfilled, there will be continual advancement. Sanctification is the work of a lifetime.[5]

These two ways of thinking about perfection are not contradictory. Our best picture of perfection comes when we keep them together. However, we must also separate them enough to recognize that the perfection Ellen White envisions for those who pass through the time of trouble is character development to the point of achieving a certain degree of spiritual maturity, of victory over sin. That is what I understand Ellen White to mean in the statements quoted above from *The Great Controversy.*

As Ellen White understood it, not only must we be perfect in this sense *during* the time of trouble; we must experience this perfection *before* the time of trouble in order to receive the seal of God:

Not one of us will ever receive the seal of God while our characters have one spot or stain upon them. It is left with us to remedy the defects in our characters, to cleanse the soul temple of every defilement. Then the latter rain will fall upon us as the early rain fell upon the disciples on the Day of Pentecost.[6]

Besides telling us that we must be perfect, in this statement Ellen White appears to say that we must become perfect on our own, through our own efforts, for "it is left with us to remedy the defects in our characters, to cleanse the soul temple of every defilement."

No wonder some of us have become discouraged and afraid! It's enough to make us chew our fingernails to the quick. Or so it seems. Of one thing we may be certain: *Adventists awaiting the end time need hope!*

I'm here to tell you that there is hope. Please read on.

A wrong solution

Before discussing the right solution to this question, I would like to bring up a very fanciful, erroneous conclusion that circulated among certain Adventists some twenty-five years ago. Those of you who were old enough back in the 1960s to be aware of the theological issues making the rounds in our church no doubt remember hearing of an Australian by the name of Robert Brinsmead. It was precisely the issue I have raised up to this point in this chapter that got Brinsmead off track.

Brinsmead reasoned that Christians will have to be so absolutely perfect after the close of probation that God's work upon their hearts in the experience of conversion, justification, and sanctification—the means for character perfection available to us this side of the close of probation—will fall short of the mark. Brinsmead decided that since these processes can't possibly make us *that* good, the seal of God will have to accomplish something special by way of perfecting our characters that was not done before. He claimed to have found evidence for this in two or three statements where Ellen White says that God's people after the close of probation will no longer be able to *remember* their sins. Here is one of those statements:

Had not Jacob previously repented of his sin in obtaining the birthright by fraud, God would not have heard his prayer and mercifully preserved his life. So, in the time of trouble, if the people of God had unconfessed sins to appear before them while tortured with fear and anguish, they would be overwhelmed; despair would cut off their faith, and they could not have confidence to plead with God for deliverance. But while they have a deep sense of their unworthiness, they have no concealed wrongs to reveal. *Their sins have gone beforehand to judgment and have been blotted out, and they cannot bring them to remembrance.*[7]

I have no quarrel with the idea that God may cause His people to forget their past sins during the time of trouble, nor do I have a problem with the idea that only those sins that have been confessed and forgiven will be thus forgotten. That is what Ellen White clearly *does mean*.

Unfortunately, Brinsmead read more than that into this statement. As he explained it, the seal of God will be a supernatural work of God upon the human mind that goes beyond conversion and sanctification in getting rid of sin. The blotting out of sin from the mind so that it cannot be remembered he took to mean the blotting out of the *sinful nature*, so that God's people will be "absolutely perfect"—whatever that means. Only thus, he concluded, can they qualify to live without a Mediator.

I was a ministerial intern in the Southern California Conference at the time Brinsmead began making an impact on American Adventism. I still remember going to hear him on a couple of occasions when he toured the West Coast. I picked up several of his books and pamphlets and studied them carefully, along with the Bible and the writings of Ellen White. This was without a doubt one of the most fruitful periods of theological growth I have ever experienced.

With the help of the Holy Spirit, who I know impressed my mind, I figured out answers to many of the questions about righteousness by faith and the nature of Christ that have plagued Adventists for at least thirty years, and the answers I reached then have stayed with me to the present time. In an odd sort of way, Robert Brinsmead was a great blessing in my life. He is one of those persons with whom I disagreed sharply, yet whose views helped me to sharpen my own.

What it will mean to have no Mediator

In the process of responding to Brinsmead, I learned some important lessons about what it will mean to be perfect enough in Christ to be sealed and live through the time of trouble without a Mediator. My ideas have, of course, matured considerably since that time, and I would like to share with you what I have learned.

What will it mean to have no Mediator in the heavenly sanctuary? I think we can best answer that question by asking the opposite question: What does it mean to *have* a Mediator in the heavenly sanctuary at the present time? What is Jesus doing for us now? Once we understand that, we can begin to understand what He won't be able to do for us after the close of probation.

Answering our prayers. The earthly sanctuary symbolized God's plan of salvation, and the ministry of the high priest within the tabernacle symbolized Christ's mediatorial ministry on our behalf now going on in heaven. That is standard Adventist theology that I trust the majority of my readers are familiar with.

One of the functions of the priest was to burn incense on the altar before the veil. The smoke drifted over the veil into the Most Holy Place, where the ark of the covenant was kept. John tells us in Revelation:

> Another angel, who had a golden censer, came and stood at the altar. He was given much incense to offer, with the prayers of all saints, on the golden altar before the throne. The smoke of the incense, together with the prayers of the saints, went up before God from the angel's hand (Revelation 8:3, 4, NIV).

According to this passage, the smoke from burning incense represents the prayers of God's people. Clearly, then, one of Christ's functions as our Mediator in the heavenly sanctuary is to present the prayers of His saints before the Father's throne.

Now let me ask you, Will Jesus continue to respond to the prayers of His saints during the time of trouble? If you take the position in the most absolute sense that Jesus will no longer be our Mediator in the heavenly sanctuary after the close of probation, then you must conclude that His people's prayers will go unanswered during that time. I trust that none of my readers wishes to carry the notion of "no Mediator after the close of probation" to that extreme.

Giving us the Holy Spirit. In John 14:16, 17, Jesus gives us another valuable insight into His mediatorial ministry. He says, "I will ask the Father, and he will give you another Counselor to be with you forever—the Spirit of truth" (NIV). It is the Holy Spirit who changes our hearts, transforming our characters into the image of Christ.

Now let me ask you, Will Jesus stop giving us the Holy Spirit after the close of probation? Will His power cease to control our lives? Will the conversion that we experienced before probation's close leave us after? That's unreasonable, you protest. But if it is true that one of Jesus' functions as our Mediator in the heavenly sanctuary is to "pray the Father" to send us the Holy Spirit, and if we press to the extreme the idea that He will no longer be our Mediator in the heavenly sanctuary after the close of probation, then it seems reasonable to conclude that the Holy Spirit, whom He gave us as our Counselor before the close of probation, will no longer be available to us after the close of probation.

Again, I trust that nobody who reads this book is willing to press the idea of "no Mediator in the heavenly sanctuary" to that extreme.

Clothed with His righteousness. Of all Christ's functions as our Mediator in the heavenly sanctuary, none is more important than clothing us with His righteousness. That this is a part of His mediatorial ministry is abundantly clear from Zechariah 3:1-5:

> Then he showed me Joshua the high priest standing before the angel of the Lord, and Satan standing at his right side to accuse him. The Lord said to Satan, "The Lord rebuke you, Satan! The Lord, who has chosen Jerusalem, rebuke you! Is not this man a burning stick snatched from the fire?"
>
> Now Joshua was dressed in filthy clothes as he stood before the angel. The angel said to those who were standing before him, "Take off his filthy clothes."

111

Then he said to Joshua, "See, I have taken away your sin, and I will put rich garments on you."

Then I said, "Put a clean turban on his head." So they put a clean turban on his head and clothed him, while the angel of the Lord stood by.

Jesus told a parable in Matthew 22 about a man who invited many guests to his wedding feast and provided them with special garments. However, one guest refused to wear the wedding garment, whereupon the host ordered him thrown out of the banquet. Ellen White explains that the wedding garment represents the righteousness of Christ, which everyone must have who enters God's kingdom.[8]

Now let me ask you this: If it is a part of Christ's ministry as our Mediator in the heavenly sanctuary to cover us with His righteousness, are we to suppose that after the close of probation we will get along without the wedding garment after all? That is the conclusion we must reach if we press to its absolute limit the idea that there will be no Mediator in the heavenly sanctuary during the time of trouble.

What does "no Mediator" mean? What, then, does Ellen White mean when she says there will be no Mediator in the heavenly sanctuary after the close of probation? Two things are available today that will not be available after the close of probation. One is the opportunity to change sides. Today God's Holy Spirit convicts unconverted sinners. This is God's attempt to get them to surrender to Him. However, after the close of probation, only those on God's side before the close of probation will continue to receive His Spirit. The Holy Spirit will be withdrawn from the wicked, making it absolutely impossible for them to be converted. Says Ellen White:

When [Jesus] leaves the sanctuary, darkness covers the inhabitants of the earth. In that fearful time the righteous must live in the sight of a holy God without an intercessor. The restraint which has been upon the wicked [the Holy Spirit] is removed, and Satan has entire control of the finally impenitent. . . . *The Spirit of God, persistently resisted, has been at last withdrawn.*[9]

112

The second thing available today which will not be available after the close of probation is the forgiveness of known, willful sin. In his first epistle, John makes it very clear that the forgiveness of sin is a part of Christ's mediatorial ministry:

> My dear children, I write this to you so that you will not sin. But if anybody does sin, we have one who speaks to the Father in our defense—Jesus Christ, the Righteous One (1 John 2:1).

The idea that the forgiveness of known sin will not be available when Christ's mediatorial ministry ceases can actually be quite frightening unless it is kept in perspective. We will discuss the implications of this in greater detail later in this chapter, so I will not go into it further at this point.

I hope that from this brief review of Christ's mediatorial ministry you have learned that after the close of probation we will continue to receive many of the benefits which His ministry provides us now. He will still hear and answer our prayers. He will still provide us with the Holy Spirit. And we will still need the robe of His righteousness to cover the sins confessed and forgiven before the close of probation. If I understand Scripture correctly, we will enter heaven with that garment, and we certainly will not dispense with it during the time of trouble!

How perfect must I be?

And now to the question that has caused so many Adventists so much anxiety: Can I be "good enough" to receive the seal of God and live after the close of probation without a Mediator? This difficulty probably causes Adventists far more stress than any anticipation of the physical hardships of the time of trouble. Yet the answer is utterly simple.

Let me begin by asking, What is perfection? Do me a favor, please, right now. Put this book down and go find a pencil and a piece of paper; then write one paragraph that defines perfection. Well, make it a page or two. Make it a book. Make it an encyclopedia if you have to! *Just tell me what perfection is.*

113

Back when I was in college, some of us theology students used to discuss endlessly the question of whether it was possible to reach the "point" of perfection, and if so, what we would be like when we achieved it. So far as I can remember, we never figured out the answer to the question. Part of the problem, I suspect, was in our assumption that there is such a thing as a "point" of perfection to be achieved in the first place. Perhaps as a metaphor of perfection—as a symbol of that happy condition—the word *point* is too limiting. Perfection is more a state of being, more a relationship with Jesus, more a way of life, than it is a "point" that one can measure to know when he has reached it. Trying to figure out what the "point of perfection" is seems to me to be rather like asking what the "point of happiness" is.

Please do not misunderstand. It is not my purpose in raising these questions to lower the standard of perfection. If anything, exactly the opposite is the case. Perfection—whatever it is—is far beyond our ken as sinful mortals to comprehend. The world's greatest neurologists have only scratched the surface when it comes to understanding how the human mind works. How are we Christians to understand what it means to have a perfect character?

The Bible itself supports this view. Jesus said to Nicodemus:

> You should not be surprised at my saying, "You must be born again." The wind blows wherever it pleases. You hear its sound, but you cannot tell where it comes from or where it is going. So it is with everyone born of the Spirit (John 3:7, 8).

It is impossible for us to understand how the Holy Spirit works in the human heart. Perfection is not what we do—though admittedly we do have a part to play in the process. But character perfection is too much the work of God's Holy Spirit in us for us to understand everything about what it means.

Let me ask you another question: Have you ever seen any-

114

one you knew was perfect—morally, spiritually, and in every other way perfect—the way God's people must be perfect to receive His seal and pass through the time of trouble without a Mediator? You may indeed have seen such a person, but I doubt you were aware of it.

Now here is the "utterly simple" answer I promised you to the question of whether we can be "good enough" to be sealed and live without a Mediator:

If you and I cannot understand what perfection is or how God's Holy Spirit brings it about in our lives, and if we can never know when or whether we or anyone else has reached this blessed state, then what business have we worrying about whether we're "good enough"?

We can never know when we are "good enough"! In fact, if I read 1 John correctly, there is something terribly wrong with anyone who thinks he can. We are worse sinners than ever if we think we are perfect. Please notice:

If we claim to be without sin [that's perfection], we deceive ourselves and the truth is not in us (1 John 1:8).

Perfection is too much what God does in us for us to understand everything about it or to know when we have achieved it. Therefore it is useless and spiritually destructive for us to worry about whether we are good enough. That kind of worry puts us on a terrible righteousness-by-works "trip"—and righteousness by works is one of the most dangerous attitudes a Christian can hold. Paul argued passionately against righteousness by works 2,000 years ago, and he would argue just as passionately today against those who worry about whether they are "good enough" to make it past the close of probation.

Our part is simply to keep coming to Him, thus making it possible for Him to work in us whatever He sees we need, and leave the question of when and whether we're "good enough" for Him to answer, not us. We discovered in the previous chapter that God will not close probation's door while there is one sincere soul still seeking to make his way into the kingdom. If perfection is largely His work in us, which we can never understand, and if He has promised that so long as we stay close to Him, He will not close probation's door till He knows we're ready, then *what is there for us to be so anxious about?*

I used to worry, too, till I learned to look at the question of perfection this way. It kept the standard just as high as ever, yet it relieved all my fears.

There is a danger in talking about perfection. There is the danger of legalism—that our "perfection" will turn into little more than dos and don'ts and adherence to rules of behavior. There is also the danger that we will look inside of ourselves for our assurance of acceptance with God instead of looking outside of ourselves to Jesus, our Sacrifice and our Mediator.

However, there is also a danger on the other side—disbelief, the failure, from a fear of falling into "perfectionism," to bring into our lives all the possibilities that God holds out to us. We will, no doubt, experience the tension between these two extremes till Jesus comes. The mature Christian uses this tension to guide him into a healthy spiritual growth that avoids the ditch on either side.

I will have much more to say in chapter 11 about how God brings us to the perfection necessary for the close of probation. And in chapter 12 I will discuss how you and I can cooperate with Him. So please keep reading. And remember that it is God's decision when and whether you are "good enough" to experience the close of probation and the time of trouble. If you continue to place yourself on His side (that's your part), you can rest assured that He won't let probation close until you're ready.

---

1. *Selected Messages*, bk. 1, p. 411.
2. *Ibid.*, pp. 411, 412, emphasis supplied.
3. *The Great Controversy*, p. 425.
4. *Ibid.*, p. 623, emphasis supplied.
5. *Christ's Object Lessons*, p. 65.

6. *Testimonies for the Church*, vol. 5, p. 214.
7. *The Great Controversy*, p. 620, emphasis supplied.
8. See *Christ's Object Lessons*, pp. 310, 311.
9. *The Great Controversy*, p. 614, emphasis supplied.

Ten

Reflecting the Image of Jesus

Have you ever watched a car speeding down the road? "That's a foolish question," you say. "Everyone has seen cars going sixty and seventy miles an hour down the highway." You're right. Every reader of this book has ridden that fast in a car many times.

Now I want to tell you something that will seem equally foolish. Do you know that if you're driving seventy miles an hour down the highway, you can't at the same time tell exactly where you are?

"I can too," you say as you speed down the highway. "We just passed that telephone pole."

But do you know that if you can tell you're by that telephone pole, you can't at the same time tell for sure just how fast you are traveling down the highway?

By now you are probably ready to throw up your hands.

Let me assure you that what I have just said is true. The reason you want to throw up your hands is that with objects as large as cars we are able to measure both their speed and their location at any one instant of time with sufficient accuracy that we are not aware of the difficulty. However, theoretically the difficulty is there, and I'm sure God is aware of it. We humans become aware of it when we try to measure both the speed and the location of tiny objects like the electrons inside of atoms. Scientists can measure the speed of an electron, or they can tell its exact location, but they can't do both at the same time. This difficulty is called the Heisenberg uncertainty principle, after the German physicist Werner Heisenberg who discovered it back in 1927.

"But what has that to do with the question of reflecting the image of Jesus perfectly?" you ask.

Quite a lot, actually. For, you see, questions exist with respect to both righteousness by faith and the nature of Christ that are difficult for us humans to understand at the same time. It seems, for instance, that when we focus all of our attention on what Christ does for us in the salvation process, we have difficulty thinking at the same time about our part; and when we focus all our attention on our part, we have difficulty at the same time thinking about Christ's part. That, I suspect, is why we tend to argue and debate these important issues so much.

Please keep the Heisenberg uncertainty principle in mind as you read about the two sides that come up, often in a very heated way, any time we discuss the nature of Christ. The nature of Christ has, unfortunately, become one of the most controversial topics in Seventh-day Adventist theology.

If you are not familiar with these issues, you may wonder what the question of Christ's nature has to do with the close of probation and last-day events. Precisely this, that Ellen White makes a number of statements suggesting that God's people must reach the perfection of Christ's character in order to receive the seal of God and pass through the time of trouble safely. Suddenly, it becomes very important to understand what Christ's perfection was like.

The following quotations by Ellen White are typical:

> When the character of Christ shall be perfectly reproduced in His people, then He will come to claim them as His own.[1]

Not even by a thought could our Saviour be brought to yield to the power of temptation. . . . Christ declared of Himself: "The prince of this world cometh, and hath nothing in Me." John 14:30. Satan could find nothing in the Son of God that would enable him to gain the victory. He had kept His Father's commandments, and there was no sin in Him that Satan could use to his advantage. *This is the condition in which those must be found who shall stand in the time of trouble.*[2]

Are we seeking for His fullness, ever pressing toward the mark set before us—the perfection of His character? When the Lord's people reach this mark, they will be sealed in their foreheads.[3]

Christians have debated the nature of Christ almost from the day that Christ rose from the grave, and Adventists are no exception. However, Adventists have the added question of what it means to be like Jesus, because that is the condition in which we must be found in order to pass through the time of trouble. There can be no doubt that questions about the nature of Christ have been intensified among us because of our view of what God's people must be like after the close of probation.

I have already explained that it is futile for us to worry whether we are "good enough" to receive the seal of God. We should no more worry about whether we reflect the image of Jesus perfectly than we should fuss about whether we are perfect.

There are three questions I would like to address in this chapter: First, did Christ have a sinful nature? Second, did He have the nature of Adam before, or after, the fall? And third, did He have sinful propensities? Anyone who thinks he can discuss these questions in print in today's Adventist Church without getting burned is probably naive, but I'm at least going to try. If you disagree with me, I hope that instead of striking a match, you'll write me a letter calmly explaining your views so that I can learn from you.

Did Christ have a sinful nature?

There can be no doubt that our Adventist pioneers taught that Christ had a sinful nature. Ralph Larson, in his book *The Word Was Made Flesh*, has thoroughly documented this point. However, since the early 1950s, when Walter Martin approached Seventh-day Adventists for information to use in a book about our church, a shift has come, if not in our basic belief on this point, at least in the way we explain it. Entire books have been written on this subject. We certainly will not settle the debate here. Nor is it my purpose to do so. I am only interested in settling enough of the question that Adventists awaiting the end time can wait with hope.

My response to the question of whether Christ had a sinful nature is essentially the same as my response to the question about whether we should worry about being good enough to receive the seal of God. *We do not understand enough about the sinful nature to answer all the questions we can raise about whether or not Christ had one.*

It has been interesting to me, as I read the various views on this question, to notice that almost without exception, people on both sides tend to take the definition of the sinful nature for granted, as though everyone understood what was meant by the term. We talk about the sinful nature, and we argue back and forth about whether Christ had one, without ever spelling out what the sinful nature *is*. I'm not sure that we can, and for that reason I'm not too interested in debating the question of whether Christ had a sinful nature.

We can argue with a thousand quotations that our pioneers believed Christ had a sinful nature, and we can call today's theological leaders in the church heretics for not affirming the same thing; but until we can provide a precise definition of the sinful nature, we really haven't done a lot more than beat the air. My guess is that the affirmation that Christ had a sinful nature was sufficient to satisfy our pioneers, but today we are asking questions about Christ's nature, and about the sinful nature, for which the simple affirmation that Christ did or did not have a sinful nature is inadequate.

I don't mind that we should discuss these questions.

Indeed, there would be something terribly wrong if we didn't! Our church would suffer for theological growth if we didn't earnestly discuss our differences. That is how we arrive at truth. What distresses me is that those who are so sure they are right often get angry with a brother who disagrees with them and call him a heretic.

If my understanding of the 1888 General Conference is correct, it was primarily this criticism and heated debate that Ellen White deplored. This heated debate, she said, prevented the Holy Spirit from entering into those meetings and into the hearts of the delegates in attendance, and it postponed Christ's return at that time. If that is true, then this same harsh spirit sometimes seen in our discussions of righteousness by faith and the nature of Christ, is still keeping us out of the kingdom today.

Adam's nature before or after the fall?

A major theological debate in Adventism today is whether Christ took Adam's nature the way God gave it to Him before the Fall, or the nature that Adam acquired after the Fall. Those who affirm that Christ did not have a sinful nature obviously prefer the pre-Fall view, while those who say that Christ did have a sinful nature adopt the post-Fall view. If you are among those who accept the post-Fall position, you may feel a bit distressed as you read my initial comments in this section, because it will probably seem to you that I am adopting a pre-Fall view of Christ's human nature. However, please do not judge me too early. Read everything I say before you make up your mind whether I am a heretic!

The following statements by Ellen White have a bearing on this question:

Christ is called the second Adam. In purity and holiness, connected with God and beloved by God, He began where the first Adam began.[4]

Christ came to the earth, taking humanity and standing as man's representative, to show in the controversy with Satan that man, as God created him, connected with the Father and the Son, could obey every divine requirement.[5]

In the first statement, Ellen White asserts that Christ "began where the first Adam began." This can only mean that Christ began where Adam was before the Fall, because she says that this beginning was with Adam's "purity and holiness." Notice, however, that Ellen White adds one important qualifier: Christ was not like Adam before the Fall in every possible way, but only in that He was "connected with God."

Now let's examine the second statement. Again Ellen White suggests that Christ began with Adam's pre-Fall nature: "Christ came to the earth, taking humanity and standing as man's representative, to show in the controversy with Satan that man, *as God created him, connected with the Father and the Son*, could obey every divine requirement."

Notice that in both statements Ellen White affirms that in some way Christ was made like Adam before the Fall, and in each statement she provides the exact same qualifier to explain what she means: "connected with God," "connected with the Father."

The expressions "union with God" and "connected with Christ" refer to the Holy Spirit dwelling in the Christian's life from the time that he is converted. As I understand it, then, Jesus Christ entered this world at birth with the same experience of union with the Father that you and I experience through the new birth. Please consider the alternative had this not been the case. We are born sinners because we are alienated, separated from God.[6] That is why we need salvation. Had Jesus been born this same way, He, too, would have been alienated from God, and the Saviour would have needed salvation. But when was Jesus born again? Ellen White seems very clear that He *never* was because He *always* was.

Some people argue that if this is true, then Christ was not made in all things "like unto his brethren" (Hebrews 2:17, KJV), because we have to be born again after our natural birth. If He never had to be born again, they say, then He cannot be a perfect example for us because He had an advantage over us. Please read that statement from Hebrews again: "In all things it behoved him to be made like unto his brethren" (KJV). It does not say that "in all things He was made like unto unconverted sinners." It says that he was made in all things "like unto his *brethren*." If the word *brethren* refers to Christians, who we can assume are converted, then the author of Hebrews means that Christ was made in all things like unto His converted, born-again brothers and sisters in the faith.

Of course, Christ had an advantage over sinners who refuse to accept God's power into their hearts! Christ held an advantage over every human being who is not born again. But the same advantage that Christ had over sinners at His birth is available to us through our own new birth.

Ellen White makes a rather lengthy statement in *Steps to Christ* that may help us understand Adam's nature before and after the Fall enough to reach some conclusions. I will quote a little at a time and comment as I go:

> Man was originally endowed with noble powers and a well-balanced mind. He was perfect in his being, and in harmony with God. His thoughts were pure, his aims holy.[7]

This refers to man's pre-Fall nature. Ellen White continues:

> But through disobedience, his powers were perverted, and selfishness took the place of love. His nature became so weakened through transgression that it was impossible for him, in his own strength, to resist the power of evil. He was made captive by Satan, and would have remained so forever had not God specially interposed.

In this second quotation Ellen White obviously speaks of Adam's post-Fall nature. Do you think Christ was like that? Did "selfishness [take] the place of love" in His heart? Was He "made captive by Satan?" Were His powers perverted?

125

But now look at this: "[Adam's] nature became so weakened through transgression that it was impossible for him, in his own strength, to resist the power of evil." While Christ's nature was not weakened through personal transgression, I believe that in taking human nature after 4,000 years of sin, it could be said of Christ that it was impossible for Him, in His own strength, to resist the power of evil. He had to conquer the same way you and I do, through the power of the indwelling Spirit. We noticed a few paragraphs back that He "came to the earth . . . to show in the controversy with Satan that man, as God created him, *connected with the Father and the Son*, could obey every divine requirement."

Ellen White says more in this particular part of *Steps to Christ* that is helpful to us in our study:

> But after his sin, he could no longer find joy in holiness, and he sought to hide from the presence of God. Such is still the condition of the unrenewed heart. It is not in harmony with God, and finds no joy in communion with Him. The sinner could not be happy in God's presence; he would shrink from the companionship of holy beings. Could he be permitted to enter heaven, it would have no joy for him. The spirit of unselfish love that reigns there—every heart responding to the heart of Infinite love—would touch no answering chord in his soul. His thoughts, his interests, his motives, would be alien to those that actuate the sinless dwellers there. He would be a discordant note in the melody of heaven. Heaven would be to him a place of torture; he would long to be hidden from Him who is its light, and the center of its joy.

If in this statement Ellen White is giving us an insight into Adam's sinful nature after the Fall, then I think we can all agree that Christ did not have a sinful nature like that. Please notice in particular that she speaks of "the condition of the unrenewed heart." An unrenewed heart is an unconverted heart—a heart in which the Holy Spirit does not dwell. I can't believe that any Seventh-day Adventist, on the left or the right, would affirm that Christ was like Adam as Ellen White described him in that last statement quoted above.

Actually, I have no problem with the idea that Christ took Adam's post-Fall nature—call it a sinful nature if you will—provided we understand that whatever it was like, He was always connected with God in the same way you and I can be connected with God. Ellen White affirms repeatedly that there are ways in which Christ *was* made like Adam after the Fall. One very well-known statement follows:

> It would have been an almost infinite humiliation for the Son of God to take man's nature, even when Adam stood in his innocence in Eden. But Jesus accepted humanity when the race had been weakened by four thousand years of sin. Like every child of Adam He accepted the results of the working of the great law of heredity. What these results were is shown in the history of His earthly ancestors. He came with such a heredity to share our sorrows and temptations, and to give us the example of a sinless life.[8]

This statement seems to describe what Christ inherited through the genes and chromosomes, through his physical inheritance from Mary. He was fully a human being, with all the liabilities that our physical inheritance passes on to us. His physical nature was like that of sinful human beings. If that is what is meant by Christ's having a sinful human nature, then I agree that He had a sinful human nature. But if by sinful human nature we mean that Christ was born separated from God and had to experience the new birth at some point after His natural birth, then I will have to say that Christ did not have a sinful nature in that sense. (See endnote 6.)

I suspect that there is adequate information in the Bible and the writings of Ellen White for us to define other aspects of the "sinful human nature" that would be useful in helping us understand what Jesus Christ was like and what we can become. Perhaps one of my readers will be inspired to take that on as a research project. I do hope that you can understand more clearly what I mean when I say that I object to the flat statement that Christ had or did not have a sinful nature—or that He had the nature of Adam before or after the Fall—without some definition of "sinful nature" or of Adam's nature before and after the Fall. Adventists for 100 years apparently could get away with using these undefined terms, because nobody was asking questions that went beyond them. But those simple, undefined statements are too subject to being misunderstood in today's Adventist climate, and I think we ought to stop using them without defining what we mean by them.

Sinful propensities

One other question about the nature of Christ that has troubled some Adventists has to do with whether or not Christ had sinful propensities. A propensity is an inclination to do a certain thing. With respect to sin, it means an inclination or a natural bent toward doing evil. The definition of *propensities* is probably as elusive for us as the definition of *sinful nature*. However, as with the sinful nature, I do not think we have to understand everything about propensities to sin in order to deal successfully with them.

I will begin our discussion of this question with a couple of statements by Ellen White:

He is a brother in our infirmities, but not in possessing like passions.[9]

Not for one moment was there in Him an evil propensity.[10]

The question is, if Christ did not have any evil propensities, how could He be an example for us who have so many sinful propensities to contend with? I have never been troubled by that problem, because I believe there is a very simple answer to it: While Christ had no sinful propensities, had He broken His union with the Father He would immediately have had all manner of sinful propensities. It was His union with the

128

Father that kept Him from having these propensities, and union with Christ can remove all of our sinful propensities. We can have the same freedom from propensities to sin that Christ had, the same way He had it. Ellen White says:

> We must realize that through belief in Him it is our privilege to be partakers of the divine nature, and so escape the corruption that is in the world through lust. Then we are cleansed from all sin, all defects of character. *We need not retain one sinful propensity.*[11]

By what means does Ellen White affirm that "we need not retain one sinful propensity"? By partaking of the divine nature. That is another way of saying, "connected with God." If we are thoroughly converted, thoroughly possessed by the Spirit of God, "partakers of the divine nature," then and only then is it possible for us completely to overcome every propensity to sin. Christ always had that experience. Had He ever lost it, even for a fraction of a second, He would have been as full of propensities to sin as we are. *Union with the Father made the difference with Him, and that is what must make the difference with us.*

The two ways of thinking about Jesus

I can sense within myself the tension between the two ways of thinking about Christ's nature. How human was He, really?

Recently I sat in a meeting with a group of fellow church members. The person in charge got off momentarily on the question of Christ's nature, and he made the statement that Christ had a nature like the angels who never fell. I wanted to pound the table in front of me and shout, "No, no, you can't say that! Jesus was like *us.*

On the other side, I have a friend who emphasizes quite strongly that Jesus was made like us in all things in order to be our example in overcoming sin. My friend and I get along just fine, but now and then he raises questions that make me nervous, such as, How could Jesus be our example in all things unless He was filled with the same selfishness at His

129

birth that possesses each one of us when we are born? And suddenly I want to jump up and down and say, "No, you can't make Jesus out to be like that. He *wasn't* like us!"

The nature of Christ confronts us with the Heisenberg uncertainty principle. Was Jesus like us? Yes. Was He like us? No. That's not a contradiction. It's a mystery—the mystery of the incarnation that we humans will never fully understand.

We will be studying the plan of salvation and Christ's sacrifice for our sins throughout eternity. Who are we to think that we can come up with all of the answers here? For myself, I try to recognize that I must live with certain tensions, certain unanswered questions, certain unresolved problems. We humans can never understand all there is to know about God. Yet we must try. We must try to see the truth on all sides and avoid getting stuck on one side.

I think the best way is to recognize that theological truth is only part of the truth and that it may not always be the most important part. As shown earlier, Ellen White emphasizes that "when the character of Christ shall be perfectly reproduced in His people, then He will come to claim them as His own." The real issue with us is to be like Jesus. It is not necessary to understand every last detail about Christ's sinful or non-sinful human nature in order to reflect His image perfectly. It is not necessary to understand every detail of His nature as it compared with that of Adam before and after the Fall in order to learn how to be like Him.

I suspect that among those who are absolutely sure that Jesus had a sinful nature like Adam's after the Fall are some who love Him so deeply, and have developed such a close personal walk with Him, that in the end time they will reflect His image fully. I am also sure that among those who "know" beyond a shadow of a doubt that Jesus' purity was like Adam's nature before the fall are some who love Him so much that they also will reflect His image fully in the end time.

It is very important that we discuss these questions, because such discussions, carried out in the right spirit, help us grow spiritually and to sharpen our understanding of issues that will carry us safely through the time of trouble. At the same time, it is not necessary to understand every theological fine point in order to receive the seal of God. People on both sides of these issues will be accounted worthy at the close of probation. Unfortunately, those on both sides who do little more than argue and debate will be on the outside when Jesus closes probation's door, not because they were wrong theologically, but because of their harsh, contentious attitude toward those who disagree with their theology of the very Jesus they claim to defend so valiantly.

Then what value, you may ask, has there been in our discussing this question at all in this book? A great deal, actually.

My first serious personal study of these difficult questions came back in the early 1960s, when Brinsmead was making the rounds of Adventist churches on the West Coast. I immersed myself in a study of these theological issues. From this study came some insights that to me were most significant concerning the way God saves human beings from sin—how He justifies and forgives us, and how He sanctifies and cleanses us. These lessons have been a great blessing to my life ever since, because they have guided my Christian experience. I will be sharing some of them with you in the next few chapters.

If we stay close to Him, studying His Word faithfully and desiring to know the truth, God will teach each of us all that we need to know about Jesus in order to be ready to receive the seal of God.

Reflecting the image of Jesus perfectly does not mean understanding every theological fine point about Christ's nature. It means coming to the place where we care as deeply about other people's pain as He did. It means coming to the place where we can weep as He did for the ignorance, the apathy, and the lostness of those we meet each day. It means coming to the place where we can forgive others the way He did when they say things and do things that thrust a sword through our hearts.

It was Jesus' union with His Father that made Him this way. *That is the only way you and I will ever come to the point of reflecting Jesus' image perfectly.* If, through the study of these controversial issues, you can come to this understanding as I did, then a study of these difficult questions will have been entirely worthwhile.

Let those debate who wish to do so. May you and I, from those same controversial issues, learn the heart of the truth that will help us reflect Jesus' image perfectly as we approach the end time.

---

1. *Christ's Object Lessons*, p. 69.

2. *The Great Controversy*, p. 623, emphasis supplied.

3. Ellen G. White Comments, *Seventh-day Adventist Bible Commentary*, vol. 6, p. 1118.

4. *The Youth's Instructor*, June 2, 1898; quoted in *Questions on Doctrine*, p. 650.

5. *Signs of the Times*, June 9, 1898; quoted in *Questions on Doctrine*, p. 650.

6. I believe that it is possible for a baby with God-fearing parents to be born, as was John the Baptist, "filled with the Holy Spirit from birth" (Luke 1:16). Such a child would be "born again" at the time of its natural birth just as Christ was, and would not be "alienated, separated from God" in the same way that an unconverted sinner is.

7. *Steps to Christ*, pp. 17, 18.

8. *The Desire of Ages*, p. 49.

9. *Testimonies for the Church*, vol. 2, p. 202.

10. Ellen G. White Comments, *Seventh-day Adventist Bible Commentary*, vol. 5, p. 1128.

11. Ellen G. White Comments, *Seventh-day Adventist Bible Commentary*, vol. 7, p. 943, emphasis supplied.

CHAPTER
Eleven

How the Refiner Works

A number of years ago I purchased my first computer. If you've never owned a computer, I can assure you that it's somewhat of an unnerving experience. A computer has a "brain" inside that works a certain way, and you have to learn how its brain works, because it can't figure out yours.

You might call a computer a giant calculator. You probably know that a calculator has a small memory that holds all the numbers you punch in, and that adds, subtracts, multiplies, or divides them according to the commands you give it on the keyboard. A desktop calculator will even print the data in its memory onto a tape. A computer does much the same thing, only it can work with letters and words as well as with numbers. When you give it a certain command, it too will print out the data in its memory onto a sheet of paper.

A calculator has one disadvantage that computers have managed to overcome. Once you turn a calculator off, everything in its memory is wiped out. If you want to refigure the problem you were working with the day before, you have to punch all the numbers back in.

Computer manufacturers have invented a way to store the

information you type, not in the computer itself, but on a disk that's coated with the same brown stuff that's on recording tape. Dump the data onto the disk before you turn the computer off at the end of the day, and the next morning when you turn the computer back on, you don't have to type the data in all over again. Just give it the right command, and it will order the disk to dump the information back into the computer's memory for you.

The computer can juggle numbers and words around for you in fast and handy ways that you could never do by yourself, and then it can either print out the information so you can see it on a piece of paper, or it can dump the information onto a disk and store it for you to look at the next day.

There are lots of other things I could mention about how the various functions of a computer relate to each other, but this is enough to illustrate the point I'm trying to make. In order to obtain maximum use from a computer, you need to understand its various parts and how they work together to accomplish the things you want to do. In the next two chapters we're going to examine the various "parts" to how God saves us, and we're going to try to understand the relationships between them. I believe that when you understand how each part of the plan of salvation works with each other part, it will be easier for you to "work with" God's plan.

As we have seen, Ellen White's primary emphasis in her discussion of the close of probation and the time of trouble is the preparation God's people must make in order to be ready for that time. She calls this preparation "perfection," or "reflecting the image of Jesus perfectly." I prefer the expression "high level of character development," which means the same thing while avoiding the absolutes that are so often implied by the word *perfection*.

There are two ways to look at character development. The first is found in Malachi 3:3, from which I took the title of this book: He will sit as a refiner and purifier of silver; he will purify the Levites and refine them like gold and silver.

Reading this statement, you'd get the idea that God was going to do the work of character refinement for us. Malachi said that *He* will refine, *He* will purify.

The other way of looking at character development is found in a statement by Ellen White that I quoted in the previous chapter. Reading this statement, you'd get the idea that character development depends on what *we* do:

> Not one of us will ever receive the seal of God while our characters have one spot or stain upon them. It is left with us to remedy the defects in our characters, to cleanse the soul temple of every defilement.[1]

Two groups exist in the Adventist Church today, representing two sides of a conflict over righteousness by faith. On one side are those I'll call the "Jesus only" group, and on the other side are the "me too" group.

The "Jesus only" people assure us that when Jesus comes into our hearts, He so transforms our natures that in due time we discover the change in our characters has already happened. It's sort of a "come along and enjoy the ride" philosophy of character perfection—or so it would seem to hear the "me too" people tell it. "That's cheap grace," they say. And maybe they're right.

On the other side, the "me too" people point to texts such as Philippians 4:13, which says, "I can do all things through Christ which strengtheneth me" (KJV). With a big emphasis on the *I*, they inform us that God provides the power, but we do the work. It's a "how can I enjoy the ride when I have to peddle so hard to keep the car moving down the road?" sort of philosophy—or so it would seem listening to the "Jesus only" people tell it. "That's a works trip," they say. And maybe they're right.

Actually, each side has an element of truth. The solution to the conflict lies in a proper understanding of forgiveness, conversion, and sanctification.

What is forgiveness?

Salvation begins with the forgiveness of our sins. When Christ pardons us, He records "forgiven" across our sins in His record books. Forgiveness says to the sinner, "Though you still

135

have some bad habits to overcome, at this moment I'm putting you right with God. You are in a saved condition. If you were to die right now, you would spend eternity with Jesus."

Some Christians are troubled by the idea that a person is forgiven and therefore saved even though he has some bad habits to overcome. "God saves us *from* our sins, not *in* our sins," they say. However, if God demanded that we overcome all our bad habits before he saved us, salvation would depend on our works, and it would no longer be by faith. But the Bible is utterly clear in teaching that we are saved by grace alone through faith, not by works. Notice what Paul says:

> No one will be declared righteous in his sight by observing the law (Romans 3:20).

> It is by grace you have been saved, through faith . . . not by works, so that no one can boast (Ephesians 2:8, 9).

The thief on the cross is undoubtedly our best example in the Bible of a man who had almost no opportunity to overcome his bad habits—and surely he must have had a lot of them, considering the punishment he received for his crimes—yet Jesus forgave him and promised him salvation.

The good news of the gospel is that once we repent, God no longer looks at us the way we really are. He looks at us according to the way we want to be. He says, "You've chosen my way of life. I'm going to treat you as though you really are that way, and then I'll help you to get that way."

In her book *Steps to Christ* Ellen White explains in beautiful language how God looks at sinners who have repented and committed their lives to Him:

> He lived a sinless life. He died for us, and now He offers to take our sins and give us His righteousness. If you give yourself to Him, and accept Him as your Saviour, then, sinful as your life may have been, for His sake you are accounted righteous. Christ's character stands in place of your character, and you are accepted before God just as if you had not sinned.[2]

136

It's Christ's character standing in place of our character, what we sometimes call "the robe of Christ's righteousness," that covers us. Zechariah had this thought in mind when he described the angel covering Joshua with clean clothes. The clean clothes were Christ's holy character standing in place of Joshua's sinful character. The person who has met the condition for salvation can *know* that he is in a saved condition *now*. If there is any doubt in your mind about whether the Christian can be sure of his salvation now, read through the entire book of 1 John and underline or highlight every occurrence of the word *know*. Then go back and study those verses carefully.

Two things must happen in a person's life, however, before forgiveness is possible. One of these is God's part. The other is our part.

God's part: Conviction. God takes the initiative to save human beings. He tries to get us to recognize a need for something in our lives that isn't there. We call this "conviction." Jesus said, "When [the Counselor] comes, he will convict the world of guilt in regard to sin and righteousness and judgment" (John 16:8). Romans 7 gives us one of the clearest pictures anywhere in the Bible of what it means for a person to be under the conviction of God's Holy Spirit. Paul says:

> We know that the law is spiritual; but I am unspiritual, sold as a slave to sin. I do not understand what I do. For what I want to do I do not do, but what I hate I do. And if I do what I do not want to do, I agree that the law is good (Romans 7:14-16).

Sinful people scoff at the idea of sin. "I'm not a sinner!" they proclaim, when from God's point of view they are utterly sinful. Paul obviously is not in that class. He admits that he is a sinner. He says, "I wish I were different." He is under conviction.

When the Holy Spirit convicts us, He tries to get us to understand that something about our life is wrong. He tries to get us to understand sin the way He does. Once we recognize the sin He's been trying to show us, He tries to get us to commit our lives to God's way. We often experience this process as

137

a very uncomfortable, guilty feeling. However, people who have been unhappy with their lives for a long time without understanding why, often rejoice when they discover God's way for the first time.

Our part: Repentance. Conviction is what God must do for a person before he can be forgiven. Our part is to repent. In a previous chapter I defined repentance as "understanding the issues of life God's way." Sinners don't do that. They think God's way is stupid. They think biblical morality is narrow and confining. But the person who understands the issues of life God's way welcomes His laws as principles that liberate, not that confine. Only through the convicting power of the Holy Spirit can we have this understanding. However, there is more to repentance than merely recognizing that the law is good and that we are slaves to sin. *To repent, a person must also make a commitment.* He must say to God, "I haven't been living Your way, but I'm putting myself on Your side. Someday I want my life fully to reflect Your plan."

Unfortunately, throughout history, millions of people who came under strong conviction never *committed* their lives to God. Many of them understood their sins as well as Paul did in Romans 7. They may even have been sorry for their sins, but sorrow is not enough. They refused to *surrender* their own way of life. Like the rich young ruler, they turned and walked away. To repent means to make a conscious choice to follow God's way of life. The repentant person will still make mistakes, but each time he will get up and say, "I know it was wrong, Lord. I'm getting back on the path with You."

There is no such thing as true repentance without a commitment to change.

Also, there is no such thing as repentance without confession. In fact, repentance and confession are two sides of the same coin. Repentance is an inward sorrow for sin, and confession is the outward expression of that sorrow. The person who truly repents will confess specific sins. Psalm 51 is without a doubt the most beautiful prayer of repentance and confession in the entire Bible. David confessed a very specific sin: his adulterous relationship with Bathsheba.

Repentance and forgiveness are as closely related as lightning and thunder. You cannot have one without the other. However, as we all know, thunder cannot happen on its own. Lightning must come first, yet when lightning strikes, thunder follows. It's the same with repentance and forgiveness. Forgiveness cannot happen on its own. Repentance must come first, yet the very instant we repent and confess, forgiveness happens.

Cheap grace is promising forgiveness to people who are sorry for their sins, but don't repent of them. No principle is more important than that forgiveness is only granted to people who fully and truly repent. Repentance is the great qualification for receiving forgiveness and the assurance of salvation. *There is no other way.*

Before we go further, I'd like to diagram what we've learned so far:

That's how it usually happens in real life. Notice on my diagram that conviction begins quite some time before repentance and forgiveness occur. When a person comes to the place that he agrees with God's principles of life and commits himself to making those principles a part of his own life, he has repented. At that very moment he is forgiven. Only one thing is missing for him to be saved, and we'll talk about that next.

Conversion

You will recall that earlier in this chapter I quoted a statement by Ellen White in which she says that Christ's character stands in place of our character, and that we are accepted before God just as though we had not sinned. In the very next paragraph she says:

139

More than this, Christ changes the heart. He abides in your heart by faith. . . . With Christ working in you, you will manifest the same spirit [Christ's spirit] and do the same good works [Christ's good works]—works of righteousness, obedience.[3]

When Christ dwells in a person's heart, he is converted. Jesus spoke of conversion when He said, "Unless a man is born again, he cannot see the kingdom of God" (John 3:3). The "new birth" and "conversion" are generally understood by Christians to be interchangeable terms. From what Jesus said, it is obvious that conversion is a necessary qualification for entry into heaven, and therefore it is a prerequisite for salvation:

> I tell you the truth, unless a man is born of water and the Spirit, he cannot enter the kingdom of God. . . . The wind blows wherever it pleases. You hear its sound, but you cannot tell where it comes from or where it is going. So it is with everyone born of the Spirit (John 3:5-8).

We need to understand several points about conversion. The most important is that through the power of the Holy Spirit, a person's inner life is transformed. Conversion creates a new way of life, not merely in the outward behavior, but in the inner desires of the heart. Paul said, "Do not conform any longer to the pattern of this world, but *be transformed by the renewing of your mind*" (Romans 12:2, emphasis supplied).

Ellen White describes this change in *Steps to Christ*:

> Education, culture, the exercise of the will, human effort . . . may produce an outward correctness of behavior, but they cannot change the heart; they cannot purify the springs of life. There must be a power working from within, a new life from above, before men can be changed from sin to holiness. That power is Christ. His grace alone can quicken the lifeless faculties of the soul, and attract it to God, to holiness.
>
> The Saviour said, "Except a man be born from above,"

140

unless he shall receive a new heart, *new desires, purposes, and motives,* leading to a new life, "he cannot see the kingdom of God."[4]

When a person is converted, the selfishness that dominated his thoughts and feelings is replaced with a desire to think of others, to be kind to them, and to treat them fairly. After he is converted, the materialistic person prefers simplicity, the proud person becomes humble, and the power-hungry person becomes submissive. All this happens, not because these people make themselves that way, but because Jesus transforms the most basic motives of their hearts, and now it is their greatest desire to be that way.

The person with a mature, well-developed character does not continually struggle against evil inner desires. The Holy Spirit has transformed his heart and replaced those evil desires with desires that conform to God's way of life. Victory over sin does not mean learning to hold the lid on the pressure cooker the rest of your life. It means releasing the pressure inside the pressure cooker. When the pressure has been released, there is no more need to hold down the lid. Similarly, when the heart has been fully transformed, we no longer need to fight constantly against sin. However, Christians will continue to experience temptation; they will have to guard against sin and cooperate with God to keep from sinning until Jesus comes.

Now let's put conversion on our diagram:

Conversion occurs just as instantaneously *after* forgiveness as repentance does before. Which comes first, the hammer striking the nail or the nail penetrating the wood? And which comes first, the nail entering the wood or the crack along the grain? Obviously, the nail cannot penetrate the wood till it is struck by the hammer, and the grain cannot crack till the nail enters the wood. Yet once the hammer strikes, everything else happens so rapidly that it seems to the observer to be all one action.

It's the same with repentance, forgiveness, and conversion. They must happen in that order. But once a sinner repents, everything else happens in such quick succession that it seems to the Christian to be all one action.

Justification: A summary so far

I would like to summarize everything we have discussed up to this point under one word: *justification*. Paul speaks of justification in Romans 3:

> All have sinned and fall short of the glory of God, and are justified freely by his grace through the redemption that came by Jesus Christ (verse 23).

> We maintain that a man is justified by faith apart from observing the law (verse 28).

In its simplest sense, justification means to be declared righteous. When we repent of our sins and confess them, God and Christ declare us to be righteous—and therefore in a saved condition—even though we still have many sins to overcome. Ellen White had this thought in mind when she wrote these words:

> In ourselves we are sinners; but in Christ we are righteous. Having made us righteous through . . . Christ, God pronounces us just, and treats us as just.[5]

I think most Adventists today would agree with what I have said so far. However, there is a good bit of controversy within our church on another point. According to one view, justification is strictly a legal transaction that takes place when forgiveness is written on the sinner's record in heaven. It is not something that happens in the sinner's heart. The other view is that justification includes both the forgiveness of sin on the sinner's record in heaven, *and* transformation of his heart through the new birth. Because of the following passage from Paul, I feel comfortable with the view that justification includes both the legal transaction in heaven when Christ forgives us and declares us righteous, and the experience of conversion in the sinner's heart on earth. Notice what Paul says:

> He [Christ] saved us through the washing of rebirth and renewal by the Holy Spirit, whom he poured out on us generously through Jesus Christ our Savior, so that, having been justified by his grace, we might become heirs having the hope of eternal life (Titus 3:5-7).

While I accept the view that justification includes both forgiveness and conversion, I am sensitive to the feelings of those who think of justification only as Christ's forgiveness and His declaration that we are righteous. I believe all parties agree that both forgiveness and conversion really happen. Both agree that forgiveness and conversion are important to being a Christian. If we had never heard the word *justification*, we could still be very adequately saved by recognizing and participating in forgiveness and conversion.

To me, then, the question of whether to think of justification as both forgiveness and conversion, or whether to think of it as forgiveness only, is a matter of definition of terms that does not affect our salvation so long as both forgiveness and conversion are real in our Christian life.

I could quite comfortably discuss justification with a person who believed that it included only forgiveness on the record in heaven, so long as that person understood that nobody is saved by that alone. Jesus said that "unless a man is born again, he cannot see the kingdom of God" (John 3:3). Conversion is as essential to eternal life as is forgiveness. If a person could be saved through forgiveness alone, without conversion, then God would be in the business of saving people whose basic nature was still attuned to sin.

In this book, I am especially concerned that you understand forgiveness and conversion as equally essential to salvation. I am not particularly anxious that you decide whether one or both fall within the definition of justification. Why, then, did I even mention the theological debate? Because in a moment it will be important to think of forgiveness and conversion together, as a unit. We will need to summarize both under one term, and I decided to let that term be *justification*. Creating another term merely to avoid the debate could be more confusing and lead to more misunderstanding than to use the existing term. So let's put justification on our diagram in the way that I am using it in this chapter:

JUSTIFICATION
Forgiveness

(Repentance) ——————|—————— Conversion

Conviction

Here's an important clarification: As I have diagramed it here, justification appears to include repentance. That is a limitation of the illustration. Justification is exclusively what God does for us: forgiveness and conversion. Repentance is the *condition* of justification, not a *part* of justification. I put repentance in parentheses to show that it is not a part of justification.

Why sanctification is important to Adventists

We are now ready to discuss the final step in the salvation process: growth in character development, or what we call sanctification. However, before we do that I would like to say a few words about why it is so important that Adventists at this time have a clear understanding of sanctification and of the difference between justification and sanctification.

Some Christians, especially Protestant Christians, have had difficulty with sanctification, because it seems to them too much like salvation by works. Sanctification is indeed "good works," but I think you will see by the time we are through with our discussion that according to the Bible "good works" are very

144

important. There is no contradiction between justification by faith and the good works that result from sanctification. Paul makes this very clear in Ephesians, where He talks about both justification and good works almost in the same breath:

> It is by grace you have been saved, through faith—and this is not from yourselves, it is the gift of God—not by works, so that no one can boast. For we are God's workmanship, *created in Christ Jesus to do good works*, which God prepared in advance for us to do (Ephesians 2:8-10, emphasis supplied).

We were *created* to do good works. Unfortunately, when Adam and Eve sinned, they broke their connection with God, and it was impossible for them to produce good works any longer. God stepped in and provided the salvation process we've been discussing in order to restore them, and us, to the place that we can once again do the good works He planned for Adam and Eve to do when He created them.

The important point to keep in mind is that good works are always a *result* of salvation, never the *cause* of our salvation. Sanctification is the process by which we learn to do more and more good works, but *even the good works that we do as we become more sanctified do not provide us standing with God.* Only Christ's death on the cross, His forgiveness of our sins, and His transformation of our hearts, can do that. The only thing God requires of us prior to the moment of justification (forgiveness and conversion) is to repent of our sins, and He provides that as a gift (see Romans 2:4). That is such an important point that I am going to repeat it in bold type:

The only thing God requires of us prior to justification is to repent of our sins.

Here's another important idea that I want you to understand:

God only expects good works from us after we have been saved, never before.

145

There's a reason why this is so important. If you think that in any way God requires you to overcome your bad habits and start living right before He will save you, then you will start looking into your own mind and heart to see whether you deserve salvation. And the moment you do that, you take your eyes off Jesus, who is your only salvation. Nothing will produce more unrest in a Christian than looking within himself, examining his own works, to see whether he is "good enough" for salvation. The Protestant Reformation began when Martin Luther learned to look to Jesus instead of himself for his assurance of salvation, and Adventists must not turn back what Luther started.

I do not want you to think that I am downgrading sanctification. I am simply trying to put it in its proper perspective. When Ellen White talks about the high level of character development that God's people must reach in order to live beyond the close of probation and through the time of trouble, she's talking about sanctification. It's at this point that some Adventists, unfortunately, have confused justification and sanctification. They think that after the close of probation it is our achievements in character development that will give us standing with God. *That is one of the worst errors an Adventist can ever fall into.* Yet over the past hundred or so years, thousands of Adventists have all but chewed their fingernails off for fear they might not be "good enough" to pass through the time of trouble. Bless their hearts, they thought their salvation during the time of trouble would depend on their high achievements in character development. No wonder their fingernails bled all the time!

I now want to state another important principle:

**You cannot achieve sanctification
if you confuse any part of it
with justification.**

Perhaps now you can understand why I am taking so much time in this book to explain how God saves us and how He helps us develop character. Any misunderstanding of that process will hinder us from making adequate preparation for the end time. I believe that is why Revelation 14:12 describes God's end-time people as those who "keep the commandments of God, and the faith of Jesus" (Revelation 14:12, KJV). These people will have a balanced understanding of the relationship between faith and works, justification and sanctification. No wonder Satan keeps Adventists quarreling about these issues all the time. He doesn't want us to be ready for the end time! It suits his purposes perfectly when we keep ourselves confused and in an uproar over the very thing—the only thing—that can prepare us to meet him on the battlefield in earth's final war.

There can be no doubt that, according to both Scripture and Ellen White, those Christians who pass through the time of trouble *must* have a high level of character development. Many Adventists have felt that the standard is too high, too impossible for *them* to ever reach. It is my desire that with the understanding you gain from the rest of this chapter and all of the next, you will regain hope as you await the end time. We *must* understand how the Refiner works. We must understand how He sanctifies us.

Sanctification

Repentance, forgiveness, and conversion all happen at a single point in time. Sanctification, on the other hand, is a long process. Ellen White says that it continues "as long as life shall last."[6]

I am now going to state a principle that is crucial to understanding how sanctification works, and also to understanding the relationship between justification and sanctification:

Sanctification is a continual repetition of justification.

That almost sounds like a contradiction, doesn't it? I just finished telling you that justification is a point in time, not a process, and now it seems as if I'm telling you that justification is the process by which sanctification happens.

And that is true.

We all know that a person does not conquer all of his sins the moment he is converted. He still has many bad habits to

147

overcome. *The way he overcomes them is to bring them to Jesus over and over again for justification.*

Suppose that the Holy Spirit brings to my attention a sin He sees I need to overcome. He keeps showing me the problem from one angle, then another, till finally I come to the place that I say, "Yes, that habit is wrong. I must give it up. Lord, please forgive me. I don't want to do it anymore." That is repentance, and at that very instant I am forgiven again.

Now the Holy Spirit begins to transform my heart on that point. Conversion has just happened again—not the general conversion that occurred when I was first "saved," but conversion on the specific sin the Holy Spirit has been convicting me of.

It's important to understand that this conversion/transformation is not completed in an instant. I may make the same mistake a day or two later, and again after that. Each time, though, I will recognize that what I did was wrong, and I'll confess it. Jesus will forgive me again, and the Holy Spirit will keep on transforming my heart. Justification happens in an instant of time. As we apply it over and over again, it also becomes a process, a way of life, that transforms our characters into the likeness of Christ's character.

That's how sanctification happens.

Please don't think, though, that each time you sin you fall out of God's grace. You wouldn't abandon your son or daughter just because he or she did something bad, would you?—not even if it were terribly bad. If you're a normal parent, you hope that your children will be good, but you keep on loving them even when they are bad. That's the way God is. The justification we receive the first time we come to Him is also an adoption certificate which makes us His sons and daughters. You don't stop being his son or daughter just because you yielded to temptation. When I say that each time you sin you need to be justified again, I don't mean that each new sin causes you to fall out of God's grace so that you are lost again. If we are truly His sons and daughters, we will repent of our mistakes as soon as we recognize them. We cease to be sons and daughters, not because we make mistakes, but because we refuse to repent of them.

Baptism and foot washing are an analogy of the point I'm trying to make. Baptism is a symbol of your first union with Christ. You don't need to be rebaptized each time you sin. Foot washing—a minor form of cleansing—takes care of that. When I say that each time you sin you need to be justified again, I am speaking of forgiveness and justification for that one sin, not of your general standing with God.

There's an important point about the sanctification process that we need to talk about next. Repentance does not remove temptation. Even after we repent of a particular sin, the temptation to do it again may be very strong. So in addition to repenting of sin, we must resist it. If this seems like holding the lid down on the pressure cooker, it probably is. The good news is that people who have been converted have the Holy Spirit's power to help them hold it down. That's what Paul meant in Philippians 4:13 when he said, "I can do all things through Christ which strengtheneth me (KJV)" So on this, the "me too" people are right.

Fortunately, there's more to the story than that. Jesus transforms our hearts, and in due time, the pressure on the inside gets weaker and weaker. This is something God must do for us. We can never do it for ourselves. So you see, here the "Jesus only" people are right too.

As is so often the case with theological controversies, the people on each side have a point, but they are so intent on seeing things from their own perspective that they are blind to what the other side is saying. Frequently, the solution to a doctrinal debate lies in finding the truths on each side and putting them together.

Now let's put sanctification into our diagram:

JUSTIFICATION
Forgiveness

(Repentance) ———— Conversion

Conviction   Sanctification

Salvation begins with conviction. You may argue with the Holy Spirit. You may try to convince Him that a certain bad habit isn't really *that* bad. Even after you agree that the Holy Spirit is right, you may resist giving up your habit. But once you come to the point of surrendering your way, confessing your wrong, and committing your life to God's way (repentance), He forgives you and begins to transform your heart. Now you are justified. However, since you still have not overcome that bad habit, He continues this same process over and over again.

Notice on the diagram on page 149 that the horizontal line representing conviction continues clear through sanctification. God never stops convicting you. Also notice that the double vertical line representing justification (forgiveness and conversion) is repeated over and over again. The long double line represents the first time a person accepts Jesus Christ, is justified, and becomes a son or daughter of God. The short double lines represent the justification that Christ applies each time a Christian asks for the forgiveness of a particular sin.

That is how the Refiner works. That is how character is developed. That is how Adventist Christians today can develop the characters that God tells us we must have in order to live through the end time.

If you've always worried that you might not be ready for the end time, I hope that what you read in this chapter gives you hope!

This is the entire salvation process. What we have discussed here has been largely theoretical. In the next chapter we will apply what we learned here to life the way we live it.

---

1. *Testimonies for the Church*, vol. 5, p. 214.
2. *Steps to Christ*, p. 62.
3. *Ibid.*, pp. 62, 63.
4. *Steps to Christ*, p. 18, emphasis supplied.
5. *Selected Mesages*, bk. 1, p. 394.
6. *The Sanctified Life*, p. 10.

CHAPTER

Twelve

Working With the Refiner

For many years I had the idea that the 144,000 was some elite group of super-saints, a club to which I could hardly expect to belong except by some sheer miracle of divine election, and whose membership it would be futile for me to make any effort to join. Then one day, reading the Ellen G. White Comments in the back of volume 7 of the *Seventh-day Adventist Bible Commentary*, I found this statement: "Let us strive with all the power that God has given us to be among the hundred and forty-four thousand."[1]

I was dumbfounded. To think that I should actually *try* to be among that group, that I ought to set that as a goal, had always seemed awesome to me. And now the awesome was real.

But when you stop to think about it, doesn't it make sense? Why should God tell us about the kind of character we must have in order to go through the end time if there's nothing we can do about it? I believe there *is* something we can do about it. The question is, What? Is it a matter of clenching our fists, gritting our teeth, and trying harder at whatever we've been doing? I think not. We need to understand the steps in the process by which God saves us and perfects us and then cooperate with Him at each step of the way. Those who do this should be able to develop their characters more easily, quickly, and efficiently.

For the past several chapters, and particularly in the last chapter, we have been laying a theological foundation that will help us understand the process of character development. In this chapter we will discuss what we can do to cooperate with God in that process.

With the knowledge Seventh-day Adventists have of the future and of the character that will be required after the close of probation, it is utterly crucial that the methods we adopt for character development be in harmony with the principles of righteousness by faith. Otherwise, we are likely to make serious errors that will retard our progress and may prevent our characters from developing to the degree necessary in order to prepare for the end time.

In the previous chapter I explained the principles of how God saves and perfects us. In this chapter I will describe methods for spiritual growth that are patterned after those principles. When we cooperate with God's plan, our character development happens more quickly and easily. In this chapter you can expect to see a further explanation of what we discussed in the previous chapter, with special emphasis on how we can work with the Refiner in our spiritual growth. Following are the points that we will cover in this chapter:

Conviction
Repentance
Forgiveness
Conversion

Since this entire chapter is about sanctification, we will not make that a separate point for discussion.

The Holy Spirit's conviction

Now and then I meet a Christian who is afraid that some unknown sin might keep him out of God's kingdom. I suspect that Adventists in particular are vulnerable to that fear, because we have been told that we must overcome *every* defect and conquer *every* sin. What if we miss spotting one? How can we be sure we've found them all?

I would like to give two answers to that question.

Let's begin by asking, Who is it that reveals sin to us? You know the answer to that: the Holy Spirit. So why not *ask* the Holy Spirit to reveal your sins to you? Since I found that statement about the 144,000 in volume 7 of the Bible Commentary, my wife and I have begun praying, "Lord, reveal to us what we need to know in order to be among the 144,000." Please notice that the wording of this prayer goes beyond merely asking the Holy Spirit to reveal sin to us. It is a request for the Holy Spirit to reveal *anything* that we need to know in order to be among the 144,000.

After saying a prayer like this, what would you expect to happen? "Well," you say, "I would expect the Holy Spirit to begin impressing me with some of my sins." That's right. So do you now sit back and wait for the guilt feelings to take over? No. The Holy Spirit has much more efficient ways of calling your attention to the things He wants you to know than for you just to relax while He impresses your mind. By cooperating with His ways, you can actually go in search of your sins, or whatever else you need to know.

The best place to begin is with your own Bible. The psalmist said, "I have hidden your word in my heart that I might not sin against you" (Psalm 119:11). As you study the Bible, ask the Holy Spirit to reveal to you what you need to know in order to be among the 144,000. *He will do that.*

Another excellent place to look for what you need to learn is in the trials that come to you. Sometimes the Lord lets us get into trouble in order to reveal our weaknesses to us. Maybe that's why Peter could say, "Do not be surprised at the painful trial you are suffering, . . . but rejoice" (1 Peter 4:12, 13). Often our trials are caused by the very weaknesses we need to overcome. If you are experiencing a trial right now, ask God to use it to reveal to you the things you need to know in order to be among the 144,000.

God may begin by revealing to you the better-known sins

such as a love for wrong sexual thoughts or the temptation to become angry, but don't overlook the less obvious sins. God might show you that you have a tendency to shun responsibility. He might show you that you are prejudiced and unkind to a certain class of people, such as people on welfare (they ought to work for a living like everyone else!) or immigrants (why don't they go back where they came from?). He may show you that you are unkind to your husband or wife or that you need to control your children more firmly or more gently or more consistently.

Perhaps God will show you that you are too suspicious, that you need to trust others more. He may show you that you are too anxious about money and things. Or He might show you that you are too careless with your things—that you don't pay as much attention as you should to how you spend money, and you aren't careful enough in keeping up your home, your car, and your furniture.

A lesson many Seventh-day Adventist Christians need to learn is their tendency toward legalism. Contrary to popular belief, Adventists are not legalists because they keep the Sabbath. Legalism is a problem for any group, who, like Adventists, encourage a strict lifestyle. The danger is twofold. First, people who maintain high standards must guard very carefully against making a religion out of lifestyle, thinking that God surely must accept them because they live the lifestyle. That is salvation by works. The second danger for people with high standards is that they will become harsh and judgmental of any Christian who does not follow their lifestyle.

I believe that more young people have been driven from the church by legalism than from any other cause. On the other side of the coin, in an effort to avoid legalism, some people throw out standards altogether, when Scripture is very clear in maintaining a high standard of behavior for Christians.

If either of these extremes is a problem with you, God is more than willing to reveal it to you. Every Seventh-day Adventist should spend a significant portion of his devotional time thinking about this problem, praying about it, and discussing it with others. Ask God to enlighten your mind to any tendency you may have the wrong way, whether it be legalism or liberalism. As you study and pray and discuss, think especially about your own life. Keep searching for ways to maintain a high standard, while at the same time showing love and kindness to those who don't practice their religion quite the way you would.

When we really get serious with God about character development, when we ask Him to reveal our flaws to us and then watch for them, it's amazing the problems He will show us that we never dreamed were there.

The first way, then, to stop worrying about the unknown sins in your life is to let God's Spirit point them out to you. Expose yourself to all the ways He has provided to help you discover them, especially Bible study.

Here's the second way to stop worrying about an unknown sin: *If God doesn't reveal it to you, don't worry about it.* If you are earnestly seeking to know His will for your life and following up faithfully on everything He reveals to you, you can depend on Him to call to your attention everything He thinks you need to know. If He doesn't bring it to your mind, you don't need to know it—at least not now.

Isn't that simple?

The reason this view is so important is that it separates God's part from our part in this whole process. His part is to reveal sin—to call it to our attention. Our part is to repent. When we try to make His work our work, we quickly get ourselves into a frenzy, wondering whether we've spotted every sin. But when we take for ourselves only the part that is ours, leaving His part to Him, and stop worrying that He might miss revealing something to us, then we remove the fear of the unknown. Suddenly the impossible becomes possible.

What a relief!

Repentance

Once God has brought a problem to your attention, you need to do something about it. You may or may not feel terribly guilty about what God reveals to you. Remember that repentance is "looking at the issues of life the way God does,"

155

which can bring either sorrow or joy into your heart. Inevitably, you will feel guilt and sorrow about some things. None of us is so perfect that we can escape that. But if God shows you a way to grow that makes you feel excited because of the possibilities it holds out for you, then thank Him and go to work developing that in your life.

As we've noted before, there is no such thing as true repentance without a commitment to make God's way our way. The important thing about repentance is not the emotional response we experience—either sorrow or joy—but *commitment*.

A number of years ago I conducted a Five-Day Plan to Stop Smoking in my church. At the conclusion, I was talking with Joan, a woman who had been quite successful in quitting. She said, "You know, Pastor, I've tried quitting before, but I always went back to it. This time I know it's for good."

"How can you be so sure of yourself this time?" I asked.

"Because always in the past I knew in the back of my mind that someday, sooner or later, there would be another cigarette in my life. This time, I know I've smoked my last one."

Joan was committed.

The problem with sin is that we love it too much. We want to hang onto it—even if it's just a teeny little bit. Commitment means making the decision that it's over with. Forever.

A very important thing happens inside of me when I really make that decision: *The desire for that sin drops by about ninety percent*! I believe that if you try it, you will discover that a firm commitment greatly reduces the strength of your desire for that special sin in your life.

An important psychological principle is involved here that God uses to help us overcome sin. We sometimes get very anxious to satisfy our desires. We can work ourselves into a frenzy of temptation just by thinking about the thing we want. On the other hand, if we tell ourselves in no uncertain terms that we aren't going to get whatever we want right now, our minds tend to accept that and cool down.

This is especially apparent with a child. If he thinks there's a ghost of a chance that mom or dad will give him what he wants, he'll wheedle and whine for hours and drive his parents nuts till he gets it. But if you tell a kid No, and he can tell by your tone of voice that you mean it, he may gripe a bit, but soon he'll be off playing happily at something else, totally oblivious to the thing he so much wanted only a short time before.

When you're having a hard time with temptation, tell yourself No in the same firm way you'd tell a kid to make him stop pestering the life out of you. Try it and see what happens.

If you wonder whether commitment is really your problem, there's a simple diagnostic test you can give yourself to find out. The next time the temptation comes on strong, say this prayer: "Lord, please help me not to do that this time." People with a high level of commitment have no problem saying that prayer. *They're looking for help.* If you have a hard time with that prayer, the chances are pretty good that you really don't want to quit. Long range, yes, perhaps, but not *this time.* But there is no such thing as long-range commitment that isn't also for *right now.* Until it's for right now, any thought of commitment is only wishful thinking.

The prayer to check your commitment is also one of your most valuable tools for overcoming temptation. I've found that anytime I am willing to pray that prayer, I overcome, and anytime I'm not willing to pray that prayer, I yield. I believe there are two reasons for that. First, this prayer is a form of commitment, a way of telling myself No! the way you would tell a kid. That, in itself, reduces the temptation a whole lot. Second, this prayer accesses God's power, which transforms your mind, cutting away the old springs of action and giving you new ones.

And now a word of caution. If you've been struggling with a particular sin for a number of years, you may be able to put this book down, make a decision, and quit just like that. And then again you may not. It's worth a try, *but don't give up if you fail.* If you aren't able to succeed at a permanent commitment just now, make a commitment for one week, or one day, or one hour—whatever time frame you feel that, with God's help, you can handle right now. Keep on making that short commitment. When you come to the place that you feel comfortable with the time you've chosen, stretch it a bit, maybe from a week to ten days, or from one hour to two.

Adventists who are serious about developing characters that can go through the time of trouble will work on developing commitment.

Forgiveness

The next step in the salvation process is forgiveness. Justification, you will recall, begins as a legal transaction that happens in heaven. God records "forgiven" across the sins you've repented of and confessed. He no longer holds them against you. Even though He's smart enough to know you did them, He treats you as though you hadn't.

"But how can I cooperate with that?" you say. "I can't go up to heaven and erase the sin myself."

That's true. That's why Jesus is there, to do it for you. The question is, Do you believe that He's done it? Or do you keep telling yourself that you're just too unworthy to merit His forgiveness? Perhaps you know that God loves you, but you think you've committed the same sin so many times He surely won't forgive you again. Or you've committed too many terrible sins even to think of getting them all forgiven.

All those ideas are lies.

With God, the real issue is not how many sins you've committed or how often you've committed them, but whether you've truly repented. If you have a great desire to grow spiritually, if you really do want to overcome your particular temptation, then rest assured that God will stay with you even through those times in the future when you slip and fall. Use each failure as an opportunity to diagnose what went wrong. Instead of whipping yourself, ask Him to help you understand. Ask Him to help you come up with a strategy that will avoid that problem next time. Then, when you gain an insight that seems helpful, act on it. All of these initiatives on your part are a sure indication that you've truly repented even if you haven't completely quit. Believe me, *God is delighted to stick by people who relate to their sins and mistakes like this.* That's the kind of person He's looking for, and He gets excited every time He finds one!

False guilt keeps many Christians from fully accepting the pardon Christ offers. The trouble with false guilt is that it *feels* so much like the real thing that it's hard to tell the difference.

There are several varieties of false guilt. One of the most common is what I call postconfessional guilt. Postconfessional guilt occurs when you've confessed a real sin, but you still feel guilty about it. Fortunately, this form of false guilt is quite easy to recognize, because once you've confessed a sin you have every right to claim God's forgiveness. Put this principle down in your little black book: *any guilt that persists beyond the point of honest confession is false guilt.* Period. The way to handle it is to put it out of your mind. Believe God's promise that He forgave you, and if you have a hard time doing that, ask Him to help you. He's just as willing to help you cope with false guilt as He is to help you with anger, lust, jealousy, or any other wrong feeling.

It is very important to understand that the mind often interprets depression, anxiety, remorse, grief, and other negative feelings as guilt, when guilt may not be the problem at all. A severe case of false guilt may be the result of a mental health problem that needs serious attention.

A number of years ago a woman in my congregation came to me for counsel. "Pastor," she said, "I just can't get rid of the guilt feelings I have."

I asked her if she had confessed her sins. "Oh, yes, many times."

We studied the plan of salvation, and I explained that she didn't need to hold onto those guilt feelings any longer. She thanked me, but a few days later she was back. We reviewed the plan of salvation again, but in a few days she was back at my door. She kept saying, "Is it really true? Has God forgiven me?" Time after time she came back, and each time I tried to impress her distraught mind that, Yes, God indeed had forgiven her.

I am convinced that this woman was suffering from a fairly serious mental health problem which she *interpreted* as guilt. Her problem was beyond my skills as a pastor to deal with, and

I referred her to a Christian psychologist for professional help.

Another form of false guilt is what I call "frivolous guilt." I had a problem with frivolous guilt myself when I was young. Along about the time I was fourteen or fifteen, just as I was getting well into my teen years, I began to feel guilty about very minor things I'd done. Maybe I turned the light back on and read a story after bedtime, or maybe I told a friend I was late to school yesterday, then later remembered it was the day before, or maybe I picked up an acorn from the neighbor's yard.

I recall on one occasion, traveling through Yellowstone National Park with my parents, we came to a sign at a particular rock formation that said, "Don't pick up the rocks." Wicked me, I picked up a stone not more than an inch across and stuck it in my pocket. My conscience fretted over that for months, till I finally broke down and mailed the government a quarter!

By the time I reached college, this had been going on for several years. I was mature enough by then that I was able to analyze my behavior. I noticed that these "sins" were always very minor, frivolous points that didn't amount to a thing. I also noticed that each time I confessed one of these "sins," within a week another one popped into my mind to take its place, and my conscience began thrashing all over again. I realized that I was on a perennial guilt trip. I still remember making a conscious decision to stop feeling guilty over anything that was frivolous. I overcame my false guilt problem in less than a year.

I realize now that I was suffering from a very common teenage malady called poor self-image, which my mind interpreted as guilt. I felt worthless, so my mind reasoned that I must be guilty, and it went in search of something objective to give reality to the feeling. I believe that I had the beginnings of a mental health problem that could have developed into something serious had I not dealt with it at a young age.

Frivolous guilt may seem foolish to most people, but to the person who is caught up in it, it is very real—and very dangerous if it is allowed to go on.

Legalism is another source of false guilt. Legalists tend to feel guilty because they ate a piece of cake or because they read a newspaper headline on the Sabbath or because they watched television. This is fairly close to the problem I had in my younger years, except that the legalist can point to life-style statements in the Bible and Spirit of prophecy to "validate" his position. Please don't misunderstand. We should be careful about the amount of dessert we eat, about reading the newspaper on the Sabbath, and about the TV programs we watch. It's when these minor points become all-consuming major points in our lives that we're in trouble.

I suspect that an awful lot of the legalism we see in the church is caused by some negative feeling in the legalist's mind such as a poor self-image or feelings of depression, which he interprets as guilt. The details of lifestyle that he picks at are simply his mind's effort to give objective reality to his negative feelings.

There are two problems with false guilt, whether it's post-confessional, frivolous, or legalistic. First, it keeps us from accepting Christ's forgiveness, and second, it gets in the way of much more important things we ought to be dealing with. The devil is more than glad to see us keep our minds in a stew over whether God really forgave that last sin we confessed or whether we ate too much sugar for dinner today, because he knows that as long as our consciences are fretting over these trivial things, we won't recognize how irresponsible we are on the job or how unkind we are to the family or how proud we are of the money we gave to the church last Sabbath.

Only God can write "forgiven" across our sins in His heavenly records. However, you and I must learn to accept that forgiveness even when we don't feel like it. We must learn to put away the false forms of guilt that so often keep us from focusing on the real problems in our lives. If false guilt is a problem with you, ask God to help you understand yourself better on this point.

Conversion

Only the Holy Spirit can change our orientation from self-

161

ishness to love. As Christians, we know that this change in our basic motives comes about through the Holy Spirit's work in our minds. We can never change our own hearts. No principle is more plain in the Bible than that.

Does this mean, then, that there's no initiative we can take to bring about this change in our lives? Is the responsibility completely God's? Are we just to sit back and let it happen? Absolutely not! There is plenty we can do. Our part is so important that I'm going to put it in bold-face type:

A consistent devotional life makes it possible for the Holy Spirit to enter more fully into our lives, causing the change in our hearts from selfishness to love to happen much more easily.

Some people have a hard time settling down to a consistent devotional life. Often, the problem is a tendency to study randomly rather than according to an organized plan. That is why I recommend a faithful study of the Sabbath School lesson. I also recommend a method that is called "journaling." Journaling simply means to write as you study.

Go to the discount store and purchase a notebook binder and some loose-leaf paper—the kind that kids use in school. Choose a book of the Bible and begin with chapter 1, verse 1. Study a verse at a time, writing out your thoughts as you go. Don't worry if they are not profound. My thoughts when I first get into a verse of the Bible are usually not profound either. The purpose of journaling is not to write profound thoughts. The purpose is to stimulate thinking. Writing our thoughts as they come to us stirs our minds into producing more thoughts. In due time, some of those thoughts will be quite profound, at least for you or me at that time.

For your prayer time I recommend two things. First, make a prayer list. Write on a sheet of paper the things you want to pray about. When you get an answer to one of your requests, write the date in the margin beside the request. Refer to your prayer list each day.

The second thing I recommend for your prayer time is that you try to focus your mind intently for one minute on one prayer topic. Do that once a day in the morning or evening. After several days, try doubling the time. A few days later go to five minutes, and from then on keep adding five minutes every now and then till you are able, at times, to pray comfortably and meaningfully for up to an hour. This may not seem possible to you now, but I assure you that it *is* possible, and when you learn how to pray like this you will have a sense of power that you have never experienced before.

Conversion is something God does for us which we cannot do for ourselves. This is the part of character development that the "Jesus only" people have in mind when they say to "let Jesus do it for you." This is what they mean when they say that when they maintain a consistent devotional life, they discover in due time that sin disappears from their lives without their even trying. The "Jesus only" people are right. Sometimes it *does* happen that way. I know, because there have been times when I experienced it that way myself.

What about human effort?

Does this mean that we should just sit back, relax, and let it all happen without so much as raising a finger? Does human effort count for nothing? That all depends on what you want it to count for. If you want your effort to count toward getting you saved, then it counts for nothing. If you want it to count toward behavior change, then it counts for quite a lot.

It seems singularly strange to me that Christians should be so nervous about good works, human effort, and trying hard for the Lord. When I go to my counselor, he encourages me to put forth real effort to communicate with my wife so that we can get along better and have a happier home. When I visit my doctor, he tells me that I really must try harder to lose weight or I may die young. My banker urges me to work hard at making a budget so I can straighten out the family finances. Later I tell my Christian friends what the counselor, the doctor, and the banker advised, and they all agree that these are very good things to do. "Work really hard on these changes," they say, "because they will help you to be much happier and get along better with people."

That night I go home and talk to the Lord about improving my life, and He says, "Son, you need to try harder to communicate with your wife. I suggest you put forth a real effort to lose weight, and I recommend that you work on developing a family budget." The next day I report to my Christian friends what the Lord said, and they all cry, "Works!"

Why is it so good to try really hard for people, but bad to try really hard for the Lord?

When you stop to think about it, the Lord does things for me that the counselor, the doctor, and the banker never did. None of them died for me. None of them will be a fraction as patient with me as the Lord is. They won't give me extra strength to follow their instructions, nor will they forgive me when I fail. I'd much rather work hard for the Lord!

As long as we understand that none of these good works counts toward salvation, I think we should try even harder for the Lord than we do for other people. So you see, the "me too" people are right. Working hard for the Lord does bring about significant behavior change in our lives.

Conquering "impossible" sins

Among Seventh-day Adventists are thousands of people trapped in sexual immorality, smoking and drinking, eating disorders, child and spouse abuse, fits of anger, and on and on. Many of these people have shed bucketfuls of tears over their sins. They feel terribly guilty, frustrated, and hopeless. The Lord only knows how many times they've tried to quit and failed. They lost count a long time ago. You can do a number of things if you're caught in that trap.

First, recognize that if you've tried repeatedly to quit your bad habit and failed, another attack on the problem probably won't work any better. I doubt that I can suggest any head-on approach you haven't already tried. I'd like to think you will quit immediately after reading this book, but I would run the serious risk of leaving you more discouraged, more battered and bruised tomorrow, if I held out hope of immediate victory. You must give yourself time to overcome this problem.[2]

The critical thing for you right now is to continue looking at your problem God's way and to continue your commitment to stay close to Jesus. That's repentance—and remember that when you repent, God accepts you as if you were already behaving according to your ideal, even though you don't always live up to it. If you keep on repenting—confessing your sins and committing your life to God's way, eventually you *will* conquer your worst sin. The following methods will help you gain the victory in due time.

Stop fooling yourself. If you've been telling yourself, "I'm in control," or, "I can quit any time I want to," then stop fooling yourself. You aren't in control. *You're a slave,* and you can't quit any time you wish. That sin has too much of a hold on you. You need to change masters.

You also need to stop fooling yourself with the idea that God is going to work a miracle to deliver you from this problem—that He's just going to take all the desire away in a day's time. He almost never does that.

Third, you need to stop fooling yourself that you can quit if God will give you just a little more strength. God will give you strength, but if you've already prayed for more strength and it hasn't worked, then the problem is not with God's power in your life but with the inadequate strategies you've been using to overcome.

Tell God you need help. Telling God that you need help seems like such an obvious step that you may wonder why I should mention it, but you really must do that as an immediate follow-up to the first step.

Tell at least one other person you need help. There's a good reason why you should tell at least one other person about your problem. It's called "accountability." Be sure you ask someone who is mature enough to deal with you patiently and kindly should you slip up. Ask him or her to check up on you once a day, once a week, or whatever other time frame you think will work best for you. Your friend may feel more comfortable making these spot checks if you give him specific questions to ask: "Have you stayed off cigarettes in the last twenty-four hours?" "Have you kept away from that woman you've been having an affair with?" "Have you maintained the diet you set for yourself earlier this week?"

Tell your friend that he should not feel he is intruding on your privacy by asking these questions, because you are giving him permission to ask them. You *need* him to ask these questions. When he does ask, *you must answer by telling the truth.*

Ask God for wisdom. There's a very simple prayer you should pray next, and you must keep on saying it, over and over as many times a day as you can remember to do so: "Help me to understand this problem." You will not notice any immediate results, but as time goes on you will gain insights that will help you deal with the situation.

Avoid profound guilt feelings. Some people feel deeply remorseful and guilty any time they yield to their besetting sin. Such guilt is nearly always compulsive. Compulsive guilt is a feeling, not a conviction from God. In fact, compulsive guilt will cover up genuine conviction from God as long as it exists. An understanding of compulsive guilt may be one of the more useful insights you gain as you ask God to help you understand your problem.

It is not likely that you will bring your major problem under control until you have learned how to avoid profound feelings of guilt and remorse each time you make the mistake. Confession is not the way to get rid of these compulsive guilt feelings. Compulsive guilt is an unhealthy feeling, just like anger or wrong sexual thoughts, and you can ask God to help you deal with it the way you would any other wrong feeling. If you have a hard time overcoming compulsive guilt, try seeking the help of a professional counselor.

Control your imagination. Instead of putting forth intense efforts to control your behavior, try working on your imagination. The imagination is the ability of your mind to see, hear, smell, taste, or feel that which is not present to your senses. You "see" yourself eating that piece of cake. You "taste" it even though it isn't in your mouth. You "hear" the words that forbidden man whispers in your ear, or you "feel" the touch of your hand on your secret girlfriend's face.

Psychology Today ran a report recently on a study that was made of impulse buyers. I was particularly fascinated by a statement made by one of the women in the study: "Once I can see [what I want to buy] in my mind," the woman said, "it won't go away until I buy it."[3]

There is no such thing as victory over a sin so long as you savor the picture of it in your imagination. Repentance is a commitment to stop *doing* something, and also a commitment to stop *imagining* it. Examine your mind carefully the next time you are under strong temptation, and you will find that in nearly every case your imagination is hard at work. You must conquer your imagination on this point before you can conquer your wrong behavior.

Maintain a regular devotional life. You must have God's continuing presence in your life to bring understanding to your mind and strength to resist temptation when it strikes. I have already discussed the devotional life in this chapter, and it is not necessary to repeat that here. The important point is that you must take the initiative to get started. There is no such thing as victory over your special temptation without a regular devotional life.

Pray instantly when you are tempted. When the temptation for your particular sin enters your mind, you have only a short time to deal with it successfully. What you do during that time is vital to your victory. My recommendation is that you do two things. First, tell yourself No! the way you would speak to a child that was getting itself into a very dangerous situation. You *are* in a very dangerous situation at the moment, and that No will have an instant effect on your desire for that temptation. It will cut a host of sights, sounds, and feelings out of your imagination. Second, send an immediate prayer to God for help. I find that when I pray at the moment of temptation, I conquer, and when I don't, I don't.

It is imperative that Adventists today put away legalism on the one hand, and the false notion on the other hand that any effort on their part is a works trip. The "Jesus only" people and the "me too" people are both extremely valuable to this

167

church. We need to get them closer together, not farther apart. It's when they get too far apart that we're in trouble!

Character development and character perfection are not bad. I get excited thinking about the possibilities that God has in store for me. And to think that I really *can* do something about it!

Higher than the highest human thought can reach is God's ideal for His children. Godliness—godlikeness—is the goal to be reached. Before the student there is opened a path of continual progress. He has an object to achieve, a standard to attain, that includes everything good, and pure, and noble. He will advance as far and as fast as possible in every branch of true knowledge. But his efforts will be directed to objects as much higher than mere selfishness and temporal interests as the heavens are higher than the earth.[4]

That, I believe, is what Ellen White had in mind when she said that we should "strive with all the power that God has given us to be among the hundred and forty-four thousand." That's not a works trip. It's a privilege. It's what we all ought to be doing anyway. The nearness of the end time just gives us a more urgent reason for doing it.

----

1. Ellen G. White Comments, *The Seventh-day Adventist Bible Commentary*, vol. 7, p. 970.

2. If you are caught up in a sin that is seriously damaging to another person, such as child or spouse abuse (physical, mental, or sexual), it is imperative that you cease that behavior immediately. You may not be able to control your problem by yourself right now, but neither can you wait to grow into self-control before you stop that behavior. You must have the help of someone who is professionally qualified to assist you, who can intervene in such a way that you will no longer harm that other person in your life. Go to a counselor, and do it today. Some states in the United States require that a person who is aware of a case of sexual child abuse report it to the authorities within twenty-four hours. If you are guilty of sexual child abuse and you live in one of these states, I recommend that you seek

the advice of an attorney first. He can advise you on ways to deal with your problem so that the legal consequences are kept to a minimum. But do not delay seeking help.

3. "An All-Consuming Passion," *Psychology Today*, May 1988, p. 12.

4. *Education*, pp. 18, 19.

Thirteen

The Sabbath and the Seal of God

Two very fine gentlemen who were members of the Church of Christ attended a Revelation Seminar that I conducted several years ago. They did not quit coming when we came to the lessons on the Sabbath. To the contrary, they seemed very interested in the subject. One evening they stayed by after the lesson to talk about the Sabbath. We visited for some time, and then I turned to one of them and said, "Can you explain to me the moral principle behind the sixth commandment—'Thou shalt not kill'?"

"Sure," he replied. "It's wrong to murder people."

"Good," I said. "And how about the seventh—'Thou shalt not commit adultery'?"

"We are supposed to be faithful to our marriage vows."

"Excellent!" I quizzed him about one or two more commandments, and then I zeroed in for the final shot: "What is the moral principle behind the fourth commandment—'Remember the Sabbath day to keep it holy'?"

"Hmmmm. Well, er, . . . uh, . . . I guess it's that God wants us to get enough rest."

That's a very popular concept today.

Another popular notion is that the Sabbath is the day we're supposed to go to church or the day we're supposed to worship God. However, a careful reading of the commandment makes it very clear that God had neither church attendance nor worship uppermost in His mind when He gave the fourth commandment. It does not say, "Remember the Sabbath day to go to church," or, "Remember the Sabbath day to worship God." It says, "Remember the Sabbath day to keep it holy."

I wish I could assure you that Seventh-day Adventists would pass the quiz that I gave to my Church of Christ friend with higher marks than he did. Unfortunately, I'm afraid that many of us would fare no better. I doubt the average Adventist would say that rest is the basic principle underlying the Sabbath. We'd be more likely to say that the Sabbath is a test of loyalty to God. And it is. We believe that it will increasingly become a test that separates God's people from the world as the end draws near. *But that still is not the fundamental principle underlying the Sabbath commandment.*

In the next paragraph I'd like to challenge your mind with two additional questions, and then we will discuss the moral principle underlying the Sabbath commandment.

A number of years ago, when I was a student at the Andrews University Theological Seminary, I used to entertain my mind with difficult theological questions. That seems to be a favorite pastime of seminarians—one that most of us continue to enjoy long after removing the cap and gown. One of the hard nuts I used to try to crack back then was this: Is there a special blessing for Adventists who keep the seventh day that is not available to Baptists who keep the first day? That was an interesting question, but the next one hit the bull's eye dead center: If there is no special blessing for keeping the seventh day, why should Seventh-day Adventists move heaven and hell to make Sunday keepers into Sabbath keepers? So . . .

What is the moral principle underlying the Sabbath commandment?

Why should Adventists try to make Sunday keepers into Sabbath keepers?

I believe that when Seventh-day Adventists understand the answers to these questions, we will then understand why the Sabbath is important—why it is the seal of God.

Since I've given a lot of thought to these questions, I'd like to share my views with you.

Why the Sabbath is important

Please turn with me to Exodus 31:12, 13:

The Lord said to Moses, "Say to the Israelites, 'You must observe my Sabbaths. This will be a sign between me and you for the generations to come, so you may know that I am the Lord, who makes you holy.' "

The King James Version says, "That ye may know that I am the Lord that doth *sanctify* you," as does a footnote in the New International Version.

Right there is the great moral principle underlying the fourth commandment: sanctification. Becoming holy. Perfection. Getting ready for the close of probation and the time of trouble.

No wonder God wants His end-time people to keep the Sabbath!

Read Exodus 31:12, 13 again, and notice that the Sabbath doesn't make us holy. Sabbath *keeping* doesn't make us holy. It is *God* who makes us holy, and Sabbath keeping is a witness to that.

When my Sunday-keeping friends tell me that Sunday is special because it's the day they go to church, I reply, "Good!"

They look at me rather stunned, as though they can't believe that an Adventist agrees with them on that, and they try again. "Sunday is special," they say, "because it's the day we worship God."

Again I say, "Good!"

By now they're totally confused. So I point out to them that

173

the Bible doesn't say, "Remember the Sabbath day to go to church" or "to worship God." It says, "Remember the Sabbath day to keep it holy." And I ask them, "Do you keep Sunday holy?"

"Well, not exactly," they reply. "We never had thought of it that way."

But again, this is getting down to the foundation of what makes the Sabbath important. And every Seventh-day Adventist needs to understand this, because if we don't, some of us will become so confused someday that we'll give up the very thing that sets us apart as God's people.

The importance of the Sabbath as a holy day goes back to the creation of the world, when God "blessed the seventh day and made it holy" (Genesis 2:3). Whatever there is about the Sabbath that's important, it was important before the fall of man, at the beginning of time when God made the human race. In fact, the Sabbath was a part of creation. God *made* the Sabbath, and He made it holy at the Creation. Yet the Sabbath is different from anything else God made. He made everything else out of matter. Even human beings are made out of matter.

The Sabbath is made out of time. It's different from all other time, but not in any way that we can perceive with our five senses. My dog and cat don't know that there's a difference between the Sabbath and other days. The birds don't understand this. Only intelligent human minds are capable of understanding that the Sabbath is holy time. That's why Jesus said, "The Sabbath was made *for man*" (Mark 2:27).

But why did God set apart this special period—one seventh of all time—for man? Ellen White explains the reason for the Sabbath:

God saw that a Sabbath was essential for man, even in Paradise. He needed to lay aside his own interests and pursuits for one day of the seven, that he might more fully contemplate the works of God and meditate upon His power and goodness. He needed a Sabbath to remind him more vividly of God and to awaken gratitude be-

174

cause all that he enjoyed and possessed came from the beneficent hand of the Creator.[1]

Analyze that paragraph carefully, and you will discover that the basic principle behind the Sabbath commandment is to provide us with time to hold communion with God, to develop a relationship with Jesus.

Now think back a moment. *Developing a relationship with Jesus is what we discussed in the previous two chapters.*

The purpose of developing a relationship with Jesus is to bring His Spirit into our hearts so that He can transform us from selfishness to love. Do you remember the "Jesus only" people and their emphasis on transformation that happens through relationship even when we aren't aware of it? Remember how they tell us that sometimes they overcome sin without even realizing it? That *does* happen to people whose hearts are filled with the Spirit—probably far more than we have any idea of. *And this can happen even more to people who keep the Sabbath holy.*

I told you in the previous chapter that a devotional life is the key to bringing the Holy Spirit into our hearts so that this relationship can happen. Most Christians understand that a devotional life consists primarily of two things: Bible study and prayer. But Adam and Eve didn't have a Bible in the garden of Eden. They didn't need one. The God who reveals Himself to us through the Bible revealed Himself to them face to face. Adam and Eve didn't need to pray in the garden of Eden, either, if by prayer we mean talking to a God in heaven whom we can't see. They talked to God face to face! Yet with all of those advantages, God saw that they still needed to devote one seventh of their time exclusively to cultivating a relationship with Him.

If God saw that holy beings who knew no sin, and who could talk to Him face to face, needed to devote one seventh of their time exclusively to building their relationship with Him, how much more do we sinful beings need a Sabbath for that purpose!

If the Spirit comes into our hearts through our relationship with Jesus, and if the power of the Holy Spirit in our hearts transforms us from sinners into saints, then what a powerful tool for transformation—for sanctification—we have in the Sabbath! That is why God told the Israelites to keep the Sabbath *"that ye may know that I am the Lord that doth sanctify you."*

No wonder the devil hates the Sabbath. Those who keep the Sabbath have a powerful tool for transforming their lives into the image of Jesus!

Now let's talk about the seal of God.

What is the seal of God?

The seal of God is mentioned twice in Revelation: chapters 7:1-7 and 9:4. Since chapter 9:4 only mentions it briefly, we will not elaborate on that verse here. Chapter 7:1-4 tells us *when* the seal will be placed on God's people (before the time of trouble) and *who* will receive it (the 144,000), but it does not tell us *what* the seal is. Chapter 14:1-5 does that, even though it does not use the term "seal of God." Please notice verses 1-5.

> I looked, and there before me was the Lamb, standing on Mount Zion, and with him 144,000 who had his name and his Father's name written on their foreheads. . . . These are those who did not defile themselves with women, for they kept themselves pure. They follow the Lamb wherever he goes. They were purchased from among men and offered as firstfruits to God and the Lamb. No lie was found in their mouths; they are blameless.

The seal of God is the Lamb's name and the Father's name on the forehead—that is, God's name written in the mind. I don't think it's so much the *name* of God that's important as it is Christ's character reproduced in the hearts and minds of those who are sealed. The 144,000 "kept themselves pure." They "follow the Lamb [Jesus] wherever he goes." "No lie was found in their mouths." "They are blameless." No wonder the Bible can say that these people have God's name and the

Lamb's name written on their foreheads. They are *like* the Father and the Lamb!

Does that remind you of anything you read before in this book?

> When the character of Christ shall be perfectly reproduced in His people, then He will come to claim them as His own.[2]

₁ The reason the Sabbath is the seal of God is not just that the fourth commandment mentions God's name, His title, and the territory over which He rules—useful as that idea may be to establish the point. The reason the Sabbath is the seal of God is that those who have the seal of God are a perfect people, and the Sabbath is one of God's most important agencies for making them that way. Notice also that the Sabbath is the only method for transformation of heart and life that has been handed down to us from the Garden of Eden.

Making the Sabbath our seal of God

The Sabbath is not, like the doctrine of the state of the dead, something we give mental assent to and then we are done with it. The Sabbath does not sanctify, it does not write God's name in our foreheads, unless we keep it. God told the Israelites, "Verily my sabbaths ye shall *keep* . . . that ye may know that I am the Lord that doth sanctify you" (Exodus 31:13, KJV).

How, then, do we keep the Sabbath?

The Sabbath is a day to be with God. It is a day to worship God, to think about God, and to learn of Him through His works. It is a day to be with God's children, to share with them the wonderful things He has done in our lives and sometimes the sad things that have happened to us. Through that sharing, both the good and the bad, we gain the spiritual strength we need for living with our trials.

The Sabbath is to be a day of joy, a day that we call "a delight." I like the way Joy Swift expressed this thought:

177

I like to rise early on a crisp Sabbath morning to climb to a rocky ledge. Here I can absorb the awesome beauty of nature around me. I watch the clouds as they roll across the endless blue sky, the trees as they gracefully bow in obedience to the gentle wind. I listen to the birds chirp cheerful "good mornings" to one another and the jay's raucous call. An eagle soars majestically above me. I am aware of the silent signs of deer and elk around me in their prints and scat. I am totally at peace, cradled in the palm of my Creator, as I speak with Him. How thankful I am for His love, for all that He has bestowed upon me, the beauty of creation around me.[3]

Joy Swift has caught the true meaning of Sabbath keeping!

How different that is from rules and regulations: "We don't wash the dishes on the Sabbath, we don't turn on the TV, we don't do our homework, we don't mow the lawn—*we don't, we don't, we don't!*" Adventists have an unfortunate tendency to think of these rules as Sabbath keeping. They aren't. These rules are useful, but only insofar as they protect us from doing that which would interfere with *real* Sabbath keeping—the kind of relationship with Jesus and the Father that Joy has learned to experience on the Sabbath day.

Rules have an important place in our lives. Children, especially, need them. Rules help teach children to live in an orderly fashion: brush your teeth after breakfast, put away your toys before you go out to play, be home by five o'clock. Adults generally brush their teeth, put away their things, and arrive home at about the same time each day, but they don't do these things because they're following some rule. They can look at the children's rules and say, "Oh, yes, I do it that way, too, but I outgrew the need of a rule to remind me of these things a long time ago."

One of the most frequent questions I get from new Adventists—Christians we call "children in the faith"—is how to keep the Sabbath. At this stage in their experience, a few "ground rules" to help them get started are helpful. If I don't bring up the subject, they'll usually ask: "Do you wash the dishes on the Sabbath? Is it OK to go to the amusement park? Can I take my family swimming?"

I try to answer these questions according to biblical principles. However, it is vital that Seventh-day Adventists explain to their new converts that the *real* reason God gave us the Sabbath is to strengthen our relationship with Him. He wants us to use the Sabbath as a way to know Him through His Word, to enjoy Him through His created works, and to serve Him through ministry to His people. Until we do that, we have only showed our converts the outer shell of the Sabbath. We have concealed its heart. And, unfortunately, the reason in many cases is that we never understood the heart of the Sabbath ourselves. *We* were only aware of the shell!

Our Protestant friends accuse us of practicing a form of salvation by works because we keep the Sabbath. I think most Adventists understand that we do not keep the Sabbath in order to be saved, but because we *are* saved. However, I wonder if the charge may not be valid in a way that many of us never thought of? If our Sabbath observance never goes beyond the level of rules and regulations, we are no better than were the Jews at Christ's time who made the Sabbath such a burden because of their rules. It does not matter that their thousand and one rules were based on tradition and our ten have a basis in Scripture. If our Sabbath observance is based on rules only, without capturing the joy of the Sabbath through the Jesus of the Sabbath dwelling in our hearts, then our Sabbath keeping is only so much salvation by works.

Once we experience the joy that can come from the Sabbath, the rules suddenly come alive. We wouldn't *want* to turn on the TV or do our homework or go to the amusement park on the Sabbath. Those activities would spoil the beautiful time we are having with Jesus on that day!

Let me ask you, Is that kind of Sabbath observance a form of legalism, as our Protestant friends so often claim? To the contrary, when we make the Sabbath a joyful opportunity to come closer to Jesus, it becomes an experience in righteousness by faith in the highest sense. The fourth commandment places the principle of righteousness by faith right in the heart

179

of the Ten Commandments. No wonder the devil hates the Sabbath! No wonder He would love to have God's own people misunderstand it and turn it into a day of all days to emphasize rules and regulations!

Why the Sabbath is holy time

One of the most significant differences between Sabbath observance and Sunday keeping is that nobody thinks of Sunday as holy time. The Puritans used to think of Sunday as holy time, and one hears of an occasional Protestant today who attempts to keep Sunday holy, but most Protestants are quick to point out that Sunday is the Lord's Day, not the Sabbath, and that they do not regard it as holy time. But the fourth commandment says, "Remember the sabbath day, to keep it holy" (Exodus 20:8, KJV).

What is the significance of "holy time"?

The word *holy* means "to set something apart for a special use." It also suggests a sacred quality, a relationship to the divine, that demands special respect. When Moses met God at the burning bush, the Lord said, "Take off your sandals, for the place where you are standing is holy ground" (Exodus 3:5). The ground was not holy the day before nor the day after, but God's presence made it holy right then, and God required Moses to show the typical Oriental sign of respect for a holy place by removing his sandals. Anytime a place, a thing, or an object is holy, we show respect for it in certain ways.

God said, "Remember the sabbath day, to keep it holy. . . . In it thou shalt not do any work" (Exodus 20:8-10, KJV). God proclaimed that a certain time was holy, and He gave specific instructions on how to show special respect for it: Don't work.

Suppose, when God first spoke to Moses at the burning bush, that Moses had said, "Oh, Lord, did You forget? There's a regular place on the other side of the mountain where I always meet with You each morning. That's *my* little spot of holy ground. I'll meet You over there in just a few minutes!"

I think you would agree that, at the very least, God would have called Moses back and said, "I told you that for right now *this* ground is holy. Take off your shoes like I told you to do."

180

Once God makes something holy, we have no right to change it. That applies as much to the Sabbath as it does to anything else. Nor is the sacredness of the Sabbath tied to the Ten Commandments, important as they are. It goes back to Creation, when God made the world and "blessed the seventh day and made it holy" (Genesis 2:3). The Sabbath was established by God at Creation for the entire human race, and there is no indication in Scripture that He ever changed His mind. This evidence appears compelling enough that one wonders why the rest of the Christian world cannot understand that the Sabbath is still holy time today. However, I would like for you to think with me just a bit more about why God made the Sabbath holy.

For the sake of the argument, let's assume for the moment that God made only one man, or one man and one woman, with no possibility for any more to be born. He might have said to them, "You choose a day for us to get together. As long as it's one day out of seven, I'll go along with it."

However, God did not do that, and the reason is that He knew that eventually there would be far more than one or two people in the world. He chose the day Himself, and told His people to keep it *as a community.*

The Sabbath is a community day—a day for corporate activity with God. Each individual is to experience a personal relationship with God on the day, to be sure; but the body of God's people are to celebrate the day together as well. This is obvious from the fact that the fourth commandment was given to the entire Israelite community.

We tend to think of the command to refrain from work as a command to each individual, which it is. But work is a corporate activity. Each person's work is related to that of many others. The carpenter depends upon the lumberyard for his supplies, the lumberyard on the salesman, and so on back to the lumberjack on the mountain. The secretaries and accountants at each office must be at work when their bosses are. The gas station attendant must provide fuel for everyone's transportation during working hours, and telephone operators must be available to assist with communication between these

181

various businesses. Each person's work is so closely integrated with that of every other person that it would be impossible for each one to establish his own special time for fellowship with God.

Seventh-day Adventists are keenly aware of the inconvenience of trying to celebrate a religious holy day that is different from the day chosen by the rest of the world. Ultimately, the only way for each individual in a community to cease from work is for the entire community to cease from work. America's history of blue laws is clear evidence that our Christian friends recognize the importance of society as a whole cooperating in the matter of a special day for religious celebration.

Jesus celebrated the Sabbath by attending corporate worship. Isaiah informs us that in God's eternal kingdom, "From one New Moon to another and from one Sabbath to another, all mankind will come and bow down before me" (Isaiah 66:23). Corporate worship demands a corporate time for worship.

Seventh-day Adventists believe that God is just as anxious for His people to celebrate a corporate day of worship today as He was at creation and at the giving of the law on Mount Sinai. He knew then that the entire community would have to agree on the day in order for it to be observed in the fullest sense as He desired. To keep them from disagreeing over which day that would be, He chose it for them. We believe that God's command for His people to set aside the seventh day for corporate celebration is as important for His entire body of believers today as it was at Creation or Sinai.

A memorial of Creation

Throughout their history, Adventists have emphasized that the Sabbath is a memorial of Creation. That this is true is evident from even a casual reading of the fourth commandment:

> In six days the Lord made the heavens and the earth, the sea, and all that is in them, but he rested on the

seventh day. Therefore [for that reason] the Lord blessed the Sabbath day and made it holy (Exodus 20:11).

What do you think would happen to Independence Day if we began celebrating it on July five?

"That wouldn't make sense," you say.

Precisely. When we change the day on which we celebrate something, we change the meaning of the celebration. That is what happened to the Sabbath when it was changed to Sunday. Sunday is not the Sabbath.

The very secular, casual observance of Sunday in our modern world demonstrates clearly that the observance of any day other than the seventh destroys the meaning of the Sabbath. The great principle behind the fourth commandment is not just that God wants us to set aside the seventh day as holy time, but that He wants us to set it aside as holy time in memory of Him as our Creator, and as a time for the entire community to fellowship with Him and with one another. He wants the entire community to find great joy in this celebration, and the infilling with His Spirit that comes through that celebration. In a sinful world, the Sabbath becomes a powerful medium for spiritual transformation. That is what makes it the seal of God.

Those who persist in establishing a day contrary to God's day are saying, in essence, "We don't want the close relationship with You that keeping Your day holy brings." I do not mean that Sunday-keeping Christians today are consciously saying that. They would surely deny any such intention. But given the meaning of the Sabbath, that is the result of their choice, whether or not they understand it.

Sunday observance, when enforced by law, is the mark of the beast, not just because it is the wrong day, but because it destroys the meaning of close fellowship with God that is inherent in the Sabbath.

The Adventist mission

We've all sat in chairs. I enjoy sitting in a chair with four legs because it provides me with stability. I feel secure.

Suppose I were to come into your home and cut one leg off each chair.

"Sitting would be harder," you say, "but I could get along well enough on three legs."

Suppose, then, that I were to cut off another leg from each chair.

"I could balance on two legs," you say.

To be sure. Suppose I were to cut off a third leg, leaving you only one on each chair.

I think you see the point. You wouldn't want me to cut even one leg off your chairs. You need them all!

God has provided us with a variety of spiritual tools by which we can initiate a direct relationship with Him. One of these is Bible study. Another is prayer. There is also fellowship with other believers.

And there is the Sabbath, given to the human race in the Garden of Eden.

Suppose it were possible for me to remove the Bible from the entire Christian community.

"We'd still have prayer, fellowship with other Christians, and the Sabbath," you say.

Suppose I could remove prayer. No Christian could pray again, ever.

"We'd still have fellowship with other believers and the Sabbath," you say.

But suppose I could get a law passed forbidding any kind of Christian gathering. Christian fellowship would be out. What do you think would happen to the spirituality of Christians if I could succeed in getting rid of Bible study, prayer, and Christian fellowship, leaving only the Sabbath as a means to establish a relationship with God?

Again, I think you see my point. Christians ought to determine never to let go of a single one of the opportunities God has given us for spiritual growth and transformation. They are all too precious!

Yet Satan has succeeded in getting almost the entire Christian community to do away with one of the most marvelous opportunities for spiritual transformation that God ever gave

184

to the human race: the Sabbath. He has even induced most Christians to ridicule those who insist on holding onto God's gift of the Sabbath and to call it legalism.

Seventh-day Adventists understand—or should understand—the true meaning of the Sabbath. Our mission is to restore to the world this beautiful gift from Jesus. We are "the repairer[s] of the breach, The restorer[s] of paths to dwell in" (Isaiah 58:12, KJV).

We understand the final conflict that is coming upon the world. We understand that probation is about to close and that anyone who wants to be ready for that time must use every opportunity available for spiritual growth and transformation, including the Sabbath. We understand that only those who insist on using *every* opportunity for spiritual growth and transformation will be able to live through earth's final conflict and remain loyal to God. We certainly cannot afford to give up the one that God gave to Adam and Eve in the Garden of Eden, before any of the others were even needed!

We also understand that Satan will do his very best to destroy our relationship with Jesus at the end of time, particularly by trying to force us to give up one of the best opportunities we have for developing and maintaining that relationship.

Our mission as Seventh-day Adventists is to keep the Sabbath ourselves, so that through it God can transform our lives and prepare us for the close of probation; to share this opportunity with others; and to warn the world about Satan's final effort to break that relationship through denying us the Sabbath which God has so graciously provided for developing it.

---

1. *Patriarchs and Prophets*, p. 48.

2. *Christ's Object Lessons*, p. 69.

3. *They're All Dead, Aren't They* (Boise, Id.: Pacific Press Publishing Association, 1986), p. 214.

Three

Living In the End Time

Fourteen

Why the Delay?

I can still remember standing by the water fountain in the men's dormitory at Southwestern Junior College one day, talking to a fellow ministerial student about the nearness of Christ's return. My friend expressed his conviction that the Lord would surely come within five years. I suggested that there were still a number of significant developments that must take place, and I doubted that five years was enough time. My friend was shocked. That anyone should doubt Christ's return within five years seemed beyond his comprehension.

That was 1957.

The year of the Goldwater election debacle I was pastoring a small church in the Southern California Conference. I happened to be a fan of Mr. Goldwater's at the time, though I doubt he ever knew it. In any event, my mind became quite exercised over last-day events, and I preached a sermon or two on "the issues." Among other things, I suggested to my congregation that Jesus might very well come within the next twenty-five years. After the service a number of the members remonstrated with me for postponing Christ's return so long.

"I only said that He might come *within* twenty-five years," I said. "It could be much sooner than that."

They seemed relieved.

That was 1964. The twenty-five years will be up by the time this book is published.

Seventh-day Adventists began preaching the return of Jesus almost 150 years ago. We are still preaching. The big question in everyone's mind is how to explain the delay. I believe Jesus is coming very soon. I, too, wish that He would hurry up and get here. I, too, watch events in the world, hoping for some development to indicate that the day is approaching. However, to ask why Jesus has delayed His return seems to me to be the wrong question. Of far greater importance is how we use our time during the delay.

Jesus gave the answer in the parable of the ten virgins. You know the story. Five girls took extra oil and five did not. The bridegroom delayed his coming, so they all slept. When he did finally arrive, the wise girls who had remembered to bring extra oil went in with him to the wedding banquet, while the foolish went out to buy more oil. By the time they returned, it was too late. The door was shut, and they were not allowed in.

If we calculate that the girls began waiting for the bridegroom at sundown—let's say at 6:00 p.m.—then by our way of reckoning midnight, the foolish girls had six hours in which to buy oil. Instead, they slept. *They didn't use their time right.*

The delay is time. Time that has been given us to use in a very specific way: getting fully prepared to meet the bridegroom. Wise Seventh-day Adventists will use their time that way. Foolish Seventh-day Adventists will not.

That's such a simple statement that it probably bores you. It shouldn't. It should alarm you. Simple things have a way of being profound.

What's most important?

The story of the five foolish virgins calls attention to our priorities. What is most important to us—this life, or the next? This life is more immediate. It's more urgent. So the urgent gets the priority in our minds over the important. It's an emotional thing even more than it is intellectual. We don't just *think* our priorities. We *feel* them.

I wish I could blow a trumpet in your ear—anything to shake up your feelings, to get your attention:

TIME IS RUNNING OUT

A lot of people say that during the delay we should put forth strong efforts to perfect character. Please read this:

Initiative is more important than effort.

A lot of Christians know they ought to change their behavior, and most of them plan to do it *someday*. But "someday" never got anything done. The only behavior change that ever occurs is the change that is initiated *now*.

I used to jog a couple of miles several times a week. I got out of the habit five or six years ago, but for the past several months I've had a growing feeling that I ought to get back to it. I kept telling myself that someday I'd start again. *Someday.* Finally, last Monday evening—just two days ago from the time I'm writing these words—I made a decision. *It's going to be now.*

I've never enjoyed jogging. It's always been something I did because I knew it was good for me. I suspect that's why I kept putting it off. It wasn't an emotional priority with me. It was more of an intellectual priority. But finally my intellect took over my feelings, and I decided that I was going to start jogging again—not next month, or next week, or even tomorrow, but *now*. I changed into my jogging clothes, and *I did it!* My wife was stunned. She said, "I can't believe it. I'm proud of you."

The only difference between the last six months and two days ago was *initiative*. God didn't make me get out there and jog. I suspect that the growing feeling I had that I ought to jog was God prompting me. That's conviction. But that's as far as God will ever go with changing our behavior until we take the initiative to repent and make a commitment. That's one of the principles we learned in a previous chapter.

191

Another thing God has been telling me recently is that I need to exercise more control over my time. That's always been hard for me to do. Time experts never made much sense to me, and I'm still not all that fond of books on time management. But for several months I've had a growing feeling that I ought to organize my time better. Recently I made a decision to do something about that. I took the initiative.

"Wait a minute," you say. "Do you mean to tell me that God expects me to achieve perfect control of my time before He'll close probation? And that 144,000 others like me are all going to have to do the same thing? Along with absolute perfection in our health habits, how we spend our money, and how clean we keep our houses and yards?"

That view of the matter misses the point of the real character development God is looking for. He does want us to achieve basic control of our lives in these areas, to be sure. But the greatest flaw is our unwillingness to do anything about these problems—our refusal, or neglect, to get started.

Perfection, on the other hand, does not mean coming to the place that your time management and housekeeping are absolutely perfect. How could anyone define that? God wants people who are anxious to develop their lives to their fullest potential. He knows people like that will manage their time right. They will keep up their health, and they will maintain an orderly house.

I can get excited about perfection like that, because it will make me a happier, more fulfilled person.

The foolish virgins were not bad girls. They were *virgins*, after all, who believed in the bridegroom's coming and were actually waiting for him. Their problem was not gross sin. Their problem was neglect: They did not take the initiative to correct a problem *now*.

Our most critical problem

The most critical problem we need to correct is that of our daily devotional time with God. Ellen White's advice is right to the point:

Those who exercise but little faith now, are in the greatest danger of falling under the power of satanic delusions and the decree to compel the conscience. . . . We should now acquaint ourselves with God by proving His promises. Angels record every prayer that is earnest and sincere. We should rather dispense with selfish gratifications than neglect communion with God. . . . *We must take time to pray.* If we allow our minds to be absorbed by worldly interests, the Lord may give us time by removing from us our idols of gold, of houses, or of fertile lands.[1]

My devotional life is much more consistent today than in the past, yet there are still days when I wish I had spent more time with God. Sometimes there's little I could have done to remove the pressures that tied up my time, but I must admit that more often than not my priorities were mixed up. I gave something first place that should have had second place. Wrong priorities are the greatest hindrance to serious Bible study and prayer in the lives of many, perhaps most, Christians. If this is your problem, do not punish yourself with guilt and try to force a change in your priorities. Priorities lie at the foundation of our character, at the conversion level, where only God can deal with them. Ask God to reveal to you your false priorities, and when He does, ask Him to change them and show you ways you can cooperate with Him in bringing about the change.

Spiritual growth of the church

Adventism in North America is in a spiritual crisis, yet very few Adventists are aware of it. We are losing almost exactly half the membership that we baptize each year, and I am talking about losses through apostasies and missing members only. When we add in deaths, the loss rate is even higher. In 1987, the last year for which figures are available as of this writing, we gained 31,138 new members through baptism and profession of faith, and we lost 15,360 through missing members and apostasies. Our growth rate was 4.35 percent of total

193

membership, and our loss rate was 2.15. It would be difficult to come closer to half than that.

If it were a matter of ignorance, then perhaps we could hope that a statistical report about this problem to our churches would bring a change. No doubt many of our church members are unaware of the true status of the church. However, I also know that quite often I hear people say things like, "We don't visit our members enough," or, "We really need to have a program to help our new members become a part of the church." Sometimes I hear concern expressed over the large number of young people we are losing. So I don't think it's totally a lack of awareness of the problem.

Then what is it? Again, the problem is a lack of initiative. Everyone says, "We really need to do something about our new members and our inactive members," but nobody ever calls together a group of people and says, "Let's design a plan." Initiative is so easy to take—and so hard. The difficulty is not that it's so hard to figure out what to do. It's that we tend to postpone, to say, "We'll do it tomorrow." But tomorrow never did a thing to initiate plans for holding our inactive members, our new members, and our young people.

Pastors sometimes take the initiative to deal with these problems, but I am convinced that until the church as a whole decides to do something, the pastor can do very little beyond his own visiting program. We will only solve this problem when the members of the church own the problem and come up with their own solution. And that *can* happen. You can visit fellow church members on your own if you wish, or if you are a leader in the church, you might wish to initiate a church-wide plan to work with new and inactive members. The problem with the five foolish virgins was that they never took the initiative to do anything. Ten thousand good intentions in churches all across North America never materialize into a thing because nobody ever decides that "I'm going to do something today, *right now*." Initiative *must* precede action.

Now is the time, during the delay, to initiate action to save souls. Tomorrow may be too late.

The latter rain

One of the most important concepts Ellen White taught in regard to the closing events of earth's history is that just before the end of time God will pour out the Holy Spirit upon His people in a manner similar to the outpouring on the Day of Pentecost. She called this the "latter rain," a term she took from the Old Testament prophets who spoke of both a "former" and a "latter" rain:

Then shall we know, if we follow on to know the Lord: his going forth is prepared as the morning; and he shall come unto us as the rain, as the latter and former rain unto the earth (Hosea 6:3, KJV).

Be glad then, ye children of Zion, and rejoice in the Lord your God: for he hath given you the former rain moderately, and he will cause to come down for you the rain, the former rain, and the latter rain in the first month (Joel 2:23, KJV).

This analogy of the former and latter rains comes from the spring and fall rains that in Bible times fell in Palestine. The former rain, at the beginning of the growing season, sprouted the seed, while the latter rain, toward the end of the season, ripened it. Ellen White compared the former rain to the outpouring of the Holy Spirit on the Day of Pentecost.[2] The latter rain, she said, would be the glorious outpouring of the Holy Spirit just before the close of probation which would "ripen earth's harvest," that is, put the finishing touch of perfection on God's people, preparing them for the close of probation and the time of trouble:

Near the close of earth's harvest, a special bestowal of spiritual grace is promised to prepare the church for the coming of the Son of man. This outpouring of the Spirit is likened to the falling of the latter rain.[3]

It is the latter rain which revives and strengthens them [God's people] to pass through the time of trouble.[4]

The significant point for our study is the relationship be-

195

tween the former and latter rains. As every farmer knows, the fall rain cannot ripen the grain without a spring rain to sprout the seed and start it on its growth. Similarly, Ellen White said that Christians must receive the converting power of the Holy Spirit—the former rain—in order for the perfecting power of the latter rain to do its work:

> Unless the early showers have done their work, the latter rain can bring no seed to perfection.[5]

I don't think there is any difference between the former rain and the latter rain as far as the "rain" itself is concerned. Rain is rain, and the Holy Spirit is the Holy Spirit. The same rain that sprouts the grain and starts it on its growth in the spring of the year could ripen it if it fell in the autumn. The difference lies in the stage of growth of the crop when the rain falls. The latter rain will be a special outpouring of the Holy Spirit in a larger measure than we normally experience it today, but it will be the same Holy Spirit. *The difference will be in our readiness to receive it.*

Those whose hearts have been transformed by the former rain will receive the latter rain, and it will bring their characters to the perfection God is looking for at that time. Those who have not already experienced the transforming power of the Holy Spirit through the former rain will not be blessed with the character perfection they need at the time of the latter rain.

Please notice the crucial importance of this idea to our study:

The significance of the delay is that it provides the time we need to prepare for the latter rain.

This underscores how important it is for us to take the initiative *now* to cultivate God's presence in our lives, for those who are not ready to receive the latter rain will also be unprepared for the close of probation. Christians at the time of Martin Luther and John Wesley could look forward to a long life in which to prepare for eternity. That is not true today.

Furthermore, we cannot look to the second coming of Jesus as the time to be ready, or even to the close of probation. We must bring the converting power of the early rain into our lives now, or we will not be ready for the perfecting power of the latter rain when it comes.

The ten virgins wake up

I would like, now, to review the parable of the ten virgins in light of what we have learned so far, together with some additional thoughts that will bring the full implication of that parable for God's people today into sharp focus.

First, I understand the coming of the bridegroom in the parable of the ten virgins to be, not the second coming of Christ, but the close of probation. The most important time for God's people in the near future is not Christ's return but the close of probation. *That* is the time for which we must prepare. Anyone ready for the close of probation *will* be ready for the second coming.

Notice, in the parable of the ten virgins, that the cry at midnight which awakens the sleeping girls does not come at the moment the bridegroom shows up. The girls are awakened a short time before with the cry, "He is on the way!"

If the bridegroom's actual arrival is the close of probation, then the cry that awakens God's sleeping church will come a short time before the close of probation. The question is, *What is the cry that awakens God's people?*

Ellen White informs us that there will be a "little time of trouble" just before the great time of trouble and just before the close of probation:

At the commencement of the time of trouble, we were filled with the Holy Ghost as we went forth and proclaimed the Sabbath more fully. . . .

"The commencement of that time of trouble," here mentioned, does not refer to the time when the plagues shall begin to be poured out, but to a short period just before they are poured out, while Christ is in the sanctuary. At that time, while the work of salvation is closing, trouble will be coming on the earth, and the nations will be angry, yet held in check so as not to prevent the work of the third angel. *At that time the "latter rain," or refreshing from the presence of the Lord, will come*, to give power to the loud voice of the third angel, and prepare the saints to stand in the period when the seven last plagues shall be poured out.[6]

Think of this in connection with everything we have learned so far. Those who have not received the early rain will not be ready to receive the latter rain when it falls, nor, if the parable of the ten virgins holds true, will they have the time to receive it when the cry goes forth announcing that the bridegroom is on the way.

What is this cry?

My personal view—and I cannot prove this, but I feel strongly about it—is that a worldwide crisis will precede, and perhaps initiate, the "little time of trouble" of which Ellen White speaks. This crisis may be economic, it may be military, it may be a terrible natural disaster, or it may be a combination of these. It may be something none of us has ever thought of yet. Whatever it is, I believe that it will be very sudden and unexpected, and that it will catch many (probably the majority) of God's people off guard—that is, spiritually unprepared for what immediately follows. This crisis will cause all of earth's inhabitants to begin searching for spiritual meaning in life, the wicked as well as the righteous. Most people will turn to spiritualism, which is already gaining rapid popularity through the New Age movement. God's people will at that time experience the latter rain, and the loud cry—the final warning to earth's inhabitants—will take place.

However, among God's people, those who are not experiencing the early rain now, during the delay, will not be able to obtain it in time for it to benefit them during the little time of trouble. We must experience significant spiritual growth now, during the delay, when everything is going along so peacefully that there seems to be no danger, for *when they finally awoke*

from their sleep and realized the lateness of the hour, it was too late for the five foolish girls to get ready for the bridegroom.
God's people today generally do not realize it, but:

We are in mortal danger of losing out on eternal life if we are not preparing right now for the crisis just ahead.

We postpone our preparation *now*, *today*, at the dire peril of our eternal salvation.

If there is one reason above all others why thousands and perhaps millions of Seventh-day Adventists will be lost when probation closes, it is that they all had good intentions to start a devotional program someday, or to get into a better health plan sometime soon. But they never did a thing about it. They are foolish virgins.

Preparing for the close of probation has taken on a bad name in the Adventist Church over the years, because all we ever talk about is how "perfect" we've all got to be. We frighten ourselves to death thinking, "I can never be that good." Unfortunately, the emphasis is too often on externals— whether we are living the Adventist lifestyle—and that quickly degenerates into legalism. Please do not misunderstand me. I believe in the Adventist lifestyle. I teach it. I practice it. It's important. But as a checklist for the close of probation or any other qualification for being a Christian, lifestyle falls far short of what God wants.

Preparing for the close of probation doesn't have to be a weary struggle. I believe the 144,000 will be the happiest people on earth at that time. They won't get that way by moaning and groaning their way to the kingdom, and if that's how you feel, then you aren't working toward perfection the way God understands it. God's perfect people are a happy people who love to sing and laugh and praise the Lord. God's perfect people spread joy and assurance everywhere they go. God's perfect people love to help others discover the same joy they have, especially those who are new or weak in the faith.

But to do any of these things, you must take the initiative

to get started. Go to the bookstore and buy that notebook for journaling. Write "Prayer Requests" over one sheet and start making a list. *Do* something. Take the initiative. Get started. Make today the best day of the rest of your life!

---

1. *The Great Controversy*, p. 622, emphasis supplied.
2. See *The Acts of the Apostles*, pp. 54, 55.
3. *Ibid.*, p. 55.
4. *Testimonies for the Church*, vol. 1, p. 353.
5. *Testimonies to Ministers*, p. 506.
6. *Early Writings*, pp. 85, 86, emphasis supplied.

Fifteen

Working for the Refiner

I f the things I have said so far in this book about the close of probation and the end of the world are true, then what do you think is the mission of our church to the world? What responsibility do you and I have to the people we work with, to our neighbors, and to others not of our faith with whom we come in contact each day? Are we under obligation, because we know about the close of human probation and the end of the world, to tell others? From a purely logical point of view, the answer to that question is Yes. The historic Adventist mission says Yes. Scripture says Yes, and if we are at all serious about obeying God's Word, the answer for each of us must be Yes.

It is quite common knowledge that Adventists in other parts of the world are taking this responsibility far more seriously than are we in North America. I could hold forth quite at length about how terrible it is that North America is so asleep. Lots of people have. I could make my readers feel guilty, under the assumption that this would motivate us all to get out and do more. But so far, every such effort has failed to wake us up or move us out to do more, and I am sure that any such effort on my part in this book would be equally unsuccessful.

I would like to share with you, not what I think the church as a whole in North America ought to do, because I don't know that, but what individual Adventists and their congregations can do.

A neighbor of mine, whom I'll call Dexter, is quite unimpressed with a well-known religious group in our city. Several years ago he and his family moved into a neighborhood that was made up almost entirely of people from this particular group. The first Sunday morning a representative from the church stopped by and announced that he had come to *take* Dexter and his family to church. Dexter thanked the gentleman for his interest, but declined. The next Sunday there was another knock. Again someone had come by to *take* him and his family to church. This went on for several Sundays, till Dexter made it clear that he was not interested, whereupon the neighborhood children shunned his children.

Recently, at a social gathering, Dexter and several others were standing around talking, when several members of this particular church joined them. "It wasn't two minutes," Dexter said, "and they had turned the conversation to the mission of their church. From then on, that's all we talked about in that group." Needless to say, Dexter is not a candidate for membership in that religious organization!

Most Seventh-day Adventists would not, let us hope, be that insensitive about sharing their faith. To the contrary, I suspect most of us are so anxious to be tactful that we are afraid to say anything to our friends about our religious faith lest we offend someone. Is there a middle of the road that is both tactful and evangelistic? I believe the answer to that question is Yes. Methods exist for sharing our faith with our neighbors and friends that will help them think favorably about us and our beliefs, and will in some instances cause them to want to know more. I would like to share a few ideas with you.

Quite often, when I see Dexter in his yard, I make a point of walking over to say Hi. Usually we'll talk a few minutes and go our separate ways. Occasionally, though, when I can see that he isn't in a hurry, I'll spend some time chatting. On one such occasion I said, "Did your parents take you to church when you were a kid?" Dexter told me that he went to a variety of Protestant churches till he was about seventeen and that he and his family still attend church once or twice a year.

A few minutes later I said, "If you were going to be strongly religious, what do you think would most attract you that direction?"

Dexter thought a moment and then said, "Probably morality." We talked about that a few minutes, and then I said, "I'm quite religious, as I guess you know. Morality is important to me, but my primary reason for being religious is that I want eternal life." I went on to explain that as I understand it, eternal life does not mean sitting on a cloud and strumming a harp all day. Life in eternity will in many ways be much like it is on this earth except for the suffering and evil. We will carry out projects that will challenge us far beyond anything we've ever imagined on this earth.

Dexter said, "I'd never thought about it like that. Come to think about it, I wouldn't want eternal life to be like a lazy retirement where you do nothing. I'd want to keep busy with goals and projects that I'm interested in." He seemed rather impressed by this new way of thinking about eternal life. We talked a few minutes longer, and then I said, "Well, I guess I'd better be going," and I left.

This conversation with Dexter was not spontaneous. It was planned. On the next few pages I'd like to share with you some methods for working with people that may help you plan a tactful approach to your friends.

Ideas for working with people individually

When I first entered the ministry, back in the early 1960s, I thought it was my duty to persuade everyone to be a Seventh-day Adventist. Theoretically I realized that many people will never become Seventh-day Adventists, but I thought I was at least supposed to try to win them over. That put a great deal of pressure on my relationships with those not of our faith, and I often felt quite uncomfortable around them. I now realize that this attitude actually hindered me in reaching the very objective I most wanted to achieve.

I have learned that Seventh-day Adventist soul winners have a much simpler objective—one that makes it possible for us to be good friends with everyone, puts no pressure on anyone, yet fulfills our mission perfectly:

Our first objective is to find people who are searching for truth.

In our relationships with those not of our faith, that's all we have to be concerned about. We do *not* have to persuade all of our neighbors that we have the truth. It is not even our responsibility to inform everyone we meet of all the truth we understand. Most of them would think it was foolish, and our telling them would in many cases drive them farther away rather than drawing them closer.

There are several progressive steps that I recommend you keep in mind as you look for people who are searching for the truth.

Pray. The very first thing you must do in order to witness effectively to your friends is to pray. And I don't mean a casual prayer now and then to "help us witness to our friends." Pray often, and for several specific things. First, pray that God will help you to be a good neighbor and a good friend. And pray that God will open the way for you to witness. Don't try too hard to witness. Wait for it to happen, and let God help you make it happen.

Friendship. Our first responsibility as Christians is to make friends with as many people as we can. My wife and I began making social contacts with our neighbors soon after we moved into our new home three years ago. We've held a couple of "block parties" where we invite everyone to our home for a social event. We've also knocked on all of our neighbors' doors several times, and some have invited us in to visit.

Friendship is the foundation for all evangelism. We should take advantage cf every opportunity for getting to know people. Each of us is acquainted with people at work. Civic affairs provide a way to meet people. When we hear of someone in our neighborhood who is in distress, we have an opportunity to help and to strengthen a friendship that may someday provide a way to share God's love.

Initiate spiritual conversations. Earlier I suggested that rather than taking the initiative yourself, you ask God to open opportunities for you to witness. Now I'm going to suggest the opposite. Once we have established a friendship, we should take the initiative to talk about spiritual things. It's tempting to think that we should simply be "the salt of the earth" and wait till others ask us. However, Christ's command to "go into the highways and byways and compel them to come in" (see Matthew 22:9; Luke 14:23) suggests that we are responsible for initiating spiritual conversations with those we want to reach, the way Jesus did with the woman at the well. If you are not used to doing it, you may wonder how to go about initiating spiritual conversations with your friends. I am still a novice at it myself, but the following methods have worked for me so far.

Whenever I'm talking to someone I would like to engage in a spiritual conversation, I begin by asking God to help me find an opportunity, and then I watch for ways to turn the conversation in the direction that I want it to go. Dexter wasn't aware of it, but I sent a quick prayer to God for guidance with our conversation. I turned the conversation to spiritual things by asking a couple of low-key, nonthreatening questions. You can nearly always get by with asking questions like "Did your parents take you to church when you were a kid?" or, "Did you grow up attending a particular church?" You will recall that I asked Dexter, "If you were going to be strongly religious, what do you think would most attract you in that direction?" There is no right or wrong answer to that question. It leaves people entirely free to answer however they wish.

People in crisis are prime candidates for spiritual ministry. Ginger is another of our neighbors. Her husband left her about a year ago. She tried to reconcile the marriage, but it has finally ended in court. Recently, my wife and I were in

205

Ginger's home, talking about her separation from her husband, and I said, "Ginger, do you think God cares about the problem you're going through right now?" That started a conversation that went on for fifteen or twenty minutes. We didn't come away with a request for Bible studies. I didn't ask the question with that in mind. But I do hope that if Ginger ever has further questions about God, she'll feel comfortable asking us.

Let their response tell you what to do next. You've initiated a spiritual conversation. What do you do next? The answer is simple: Stop talking and see if they continue the conversation. That's how you find out who is searching for truth. People who are interested in spiritual things will keep talking. People who aren't, won't. If they don't pick up within a few seconds on the spiritual point you brought up, turn the conversation to something else yourself. That lets them know you aren't trying to push your religion on them, which will make it easier for them to continue being friends with you.

It will take a tremendous pressure off your soul-winning efforts when you learn this principle:

Let their response tell you what to do next.

This principle should follow through all of your soul-winning efforts, from beginning to end. *Always let them tell you what to do next.* Usually they will not be aware that they are telling you what to do next. It's more subtle than that. You must do and say things that will give them a chance to signal you.

What to do when someone is quite interested. Occasionally you will find someone who shows quite an interest in spiritual things, and perhaps even in our faith. The best way to handle that is to take an initiative that leaves them free to tell you how far and how fast they want to go. Ask "would you like" questions that leave them in charge of the situation. For instance, if they ask quite a few questions about the Sabbath or one of our other beliefs, you might say, "I can tell that you really are interested in this subject. *Would you like* for me to

206

bring you a magazine article or a small book on that subject?" If they say Yes, find something in the next few days and give it to them.

Occasionally you'll find people who are so interested in the Adventist faith that they'll ask you one question after another about all kinds of things. This is a good sign that you have found someone who is ready for Bible studies. Again, ask a "would you like" question. You might say, "I'm really glad you're so interested in spiritual things. *Would you like to study the Bible together?*"

Pray all the time. Pray each day that God will lead you to someone who is searching for the truth and that He will give you tact and wisdom to know how to respond when you do find someone like that. When you are with people, keep praying for openings to initiate a spiritual point into the conversation. Ask God to give you just the right words to say and the right way to say them. You initiate friendships and low-key discussions on spiritual things. From there, be quiet and trust God to lead you to souls who are searching for the truth. He is anxious to cooperate with you in that kind of work!

Ideas for working with people as a church

We are responsible, not only as individuals to work with our friends, but as a church to reach into our communities with our message. Friendship and the simple, low-key ways I've mentioned for talking to friends about spiritual things should be the foundation of any such group efforts. I suggest the following simple things your church as a whole can do to enhance its evangelistic effectiveness.

Each year, thousands of non-Adventist guests walk through the doors of our churches in North America. In most instances I'm sure we shake their hands and welcome them to our services—and not much more. Yet among these guests are hundreds if not thousands who would join our churches if someone found out who they are and where they live, and then went to see them.

Unfortunately, most churches do not have an efficient method for getting in touch with these people after they leave our services. The average Adventist church has a guest book, to be sure, but most visitors will write only their name and their hometown. They will not usually give their address, and never their phone number. Guest books don't ask for that important bit of information! Furthermore, the names in guest books are difficult to organize and sort. If they are to be useful at all, someone must copy them onto cards.

So begin your church's evangelistic outreach by designing a 4" x 6" guest card. For a nominal price, a local print shop can set the type and print a thousand or so on twenty-pound colored stock, made up into pads of fifty. Ninety percent of your guests will fill out this card in its entirety, including their phone number, without batting an eyelash.

You should also train greeters to spot guests and invite them to sign a card. Instruct your greeters to engage each guest in a friendly conversation, help them to find Sabbath School departments, if necessary, and listen for meaningful comments such as, "My mother was a Seventh-day Adventist," or, "We've been reading about the Sabbath and just decided to try your church out." The greeters should make a note of these comments on the back of the guest card. At least one greeter should be at the door from half an hour before Sabbath School begins until at least fifteen minutes into the worship service. Guests often arrive that late.

Next, organize a team of three or four people to visit these guests in their homes. I recommend that you make a home visit to each guest who attends your church. Try to make these calls within one week of the day they attend—two at the most.

This same team can also contact many or all of the other interests who come to the church's attention. Our larger churches receive several hundred names a year from Adventist radio and television ministries; literature evangelists' paid-out accounts; *Signs of the Times*, *El Centinela*, and *Message* magazine subscription lists, etc. For the most part, I do not recommend that you try to visit these people in their homes. Except in the case of those you know to be very interested in our message, it is a waste of time to drive all over the place to call on names from media sources, missionary journals, etc. It is much more efficient, and just as effective, to call these people on the telephone. Only drive out to see those whose telephone numbers you cannot find or whom you discover to be more than casual interests.

Each time you make a contact, you should have a plan in the back of your mind for some way to advance that person's knowledge of our message. For guests who attend church and for first-time names from media sources such as "It Is Written" or "Quiet Hour", I usually offer a year's subscription to *Signs, Message,* or *El Centinela.* These journals are an attractive, nonthreatening way to introduce people to our message once a month at a very low cost.

If I know that someone has had the opportunity of meaningful exposure to our message (persons who have purchased our literature or who have received a missionary journal for at least a year), I offer a series of Bible study guides. However, you will quickly discover, if you get very many people going on Bible study guides, that you do not have enough personnel in your church to handle the demand. For that reason, I offer the Voice of Prophecy's New Life study guides to all Bible study requests except those I know are seriously interested in our message. Your most serious interests should receive some form of personal instruction, either individually or in study groups.

Develop an evangelism master plan for your church

Each Seventh-day Adventist Church needs to have a master plan for evangelizing its community. It is imperative that this master plan be developed by the church as a whole, not just by the pastor and a few members.

It is also imperative that we stretch our imaginations far beyond what we are accustomed to thinking as we make long-range plans for evangelism. The task God has assigned this church demands a total mobilization of our personnel and our financial resources during the next few years. What I say next will probably startle you, but it is so important that I am going to state it in bold face:

209

I am convinced that in most Adventist churches the members generate enough money through their personal income that they could easily, as a church, invest $20,000 a year in evangelism for each 100 members. That's only $200 per member. Some members could not give that much, but many could contribute much more. Churches of 250 members should be able to generate $50,000 a year, churches of 500 members $100,000 a year, and so on. Most Adventist churches in North America have the resources to sustain this level of giving to evangelism over a period of many years and still maintain their church expense and their church school expense funds.

You may think that my "statistics" are unrealistic. Given the present level of spirituality and commitment in most Adventist churches, and the present level of awareness by the average Seventh-day Adventist as to what constitutes our church's mission, you are almost certainly correct. However, money is not the problem. We *have* the money. We do *not* have the vision, the sense of mission, or the commitment. But given the nearness of the end and our understanding of the mission God has charged us with, how can we think any smaller than that! If we really get serious with our personal lives and with using our financial resources for the Lord, He will multiply these meager figures many times over.

How should that kind of money be spent? There are lots of possibilities. Here are just a few suggestions:

- Mass advertising such as radio and TV spots, highway and city billboards, placards on the sides of buses, etc.
- Seminars on marriage, parenting, health, grief recovery, money management, etc.
- Community-service buildings and welfare services on a scale far more broad than most churches ever thought of, to meet the needs of people in distress.
- Demographic studies to determine the kinds of people

who live in each area of a city and the best methods for attracting each segment of the population to our message.

- Mass mailings to specific people groups within cities, with each group targeted to receive a piece especially designed to address its interests and needs.
- Sponsorship of our radio and TV programs during peak listening and viewing hours, with response opportunities built in, and enough members trained to handle the flood of requests that can be anticipated.
- Weekend Bible seminars, done with the highest level of professionalism and conducted in attractive facilities such as large hotel banquet rooms.
- Extensive use of *Signs of the Times*, *Message* magazine, and *El Centinela*.

There are scores of ways to do large scale-evangelism. With careful advance planning and faithful follow-up of each person who shows an interest, we can maximize the results. Goals should be set, with specific plans for meeting them, and accountability required of those in charge of each program.

However, we must never allow methods and goals to blind us to the real mission of the Seventh-day Adventist Church at this hour in history. Baptisms, financial objectives, and magazine subscriptions are one valid way to measure the success of a program, but only one way, and not the most important way.

Our real objective is to prepare people spiritually for the close of probation and the time of trouble, so that they can be ready to meet Jesus when He comes. Our real goal is to help people develop a close personal relationship with Jesus. We must teach them the principles of righteousness by faith so clearly that they understand how to trust Jesus for salvation, while at the same time developing a character that will stand the test of earth's final trial. We must understand these things by personal experience ourselves, and we must develop methods for communicating them to large numbers of people at one time, because in the near future that is ex-

211

actly what we will have to do if our understanding of last-day events is correct.

Lay participation

Perhaps you noticed that I've said very little in this chapter about traditional forms of public evangelism such as crusades and Revelation seminars. That is not because I am opposed to them, but because these forms of evangelism are usually conducted by the pastor or an evangelist, with the church members acting as supporters and spectators. Often, the initiative for traditional methods of evangelism comes from the conference, and the members in the churches see it as simply "another program."

I am convinced that until large numbers of church members take a personal initiative to carry our message to North America, the task will not get done. North America *will* experience the same success we are seeing in other parts of the world when we follow their method of lay participation. Ellen White suggests that this will happen when God's people receive the latter rain:

> They [God's people] will declare the truth with the might of the Spirit's power. Multitudes will receive the faith and join the armies of the Lord.[1]

> During the loud cry, the church, aided by the providential interpositions of her exalted Lord, will diffuse the knowledge of salvation so abundantly that light will be communicated to every city and town. The earth will be filled with the knowledge of salvation.[2]

I honestly get excited thinking about what is coming. Ellen White predicted a worldwide finishing of the work on a grand scale that we have never dreamed of. This work will often be carried out in the face of intense opposition and at great personal sacrifice, both on the part of the workers and those supporting their work financially. But under the power of the Holy Spirit *it will be done.*

You may be tempted to say, "Let's just wait for the latter rain, and then we'll all get busy and work." However, I suspect that the present lethargy among North American Adventists is not so much a sign that we do not have the *latter* rain as it is a sign that we do not have the *former* rain. Ellen White compares the former rain to Pentecost, and look at the evangelism explosion that occurred then!

Only those taking the initiative to bring the early rain into their lives *now* will receive the power of the latter rain to help finish God's work *then*. The preaching of the gospel under the power of the latter rain will bring persecution to God's people. I suspect that many lukewarm Seventh-day Adventists, who have not received either the former or the latter rain, will complain that their Spirit-filled brothers and sisters are bringing trouble onto the church. Some of these will leave us. That will be the most dreadful fulfillment of Jesus' warning about the foolish virgins.

But let's get back to the positive side. I like something that King David said in the Psalms:

> Restore to me the joy of your salvation and grant me a willing spirit, to sustain me. Then will I teach transgressors your ways, and sinners will turn back to you (Psalm 51:12, 13).

Did you read that carefully? When we know the joy of God's salvation and when we have His Spirit in our hearts to sustain us, then, and only then, will we be able to teach transgressors His ways and turn sinners back to Him. *Evangelism is impossible without the power of the Holy Spirit in our hearts*. That is why lukewarm Laodicean Adventists in North America so desperately need the Holy Spirit. We really cannot discuss evangelism meaningfully apart from that, because Seventh-day Adventist outreach to the world just before Jesus comes will have the power of the Holy Spirit behind it.

Billions of people must yet be warned. We cannot possibly carry out such a monumental task alone. We *must* have God's Spirit in latter-rain power to achieve the task. But God can only pour out His Spirit on people.

Does He have people in North America willing to receive His Spirit and do His work? I believe He does. I want to be one of those people whom He can use to finish the task.

Do you?

_____

1. *Evangelism*, p. 700.
2. *Ibid.*, p. 694.

CHAPTER

Sixteen

A Time to Decide

Adventism is changing. That is inevitable. Life is a constant change. Adventism's change in North America during the last 100 years has been toward adaptation to the North American culture, which is increasingly materialistic and secular. Adventists are becoming materialistic and secular, to the point that religion for many of us has become a one-day-a-week affair.

But is change toward the secular inevitable and irresistible? The answer to that question is a positive No. We are not doomed to slide downhill. Evangelical Christianity in North America is experiencing a resurgence of power that is making a marked and growing impact on the American scene. In the United States, the Republican party has been forced to give at least lip service to the agenda of the religious right.

Secularism still holds a powerful influence over our social institutions, particularly over our educational and communications institutions. Yet these are being forced to recognize the growing fundamentalist influence on our society. They may ridicule fundamentalists. But the point is that they can no longer ignore them. Evangelicals and fundamentalists in North America *are* revitalized, and they *are* being heard.

Adventism too?

There isn't a reason in the world why a similar revitalization cannot happen to Adventism in North America. Indeed, I believe that it *will* happen. A look at evangelical Protestantism outside our church suggests some patterns that Adventists concerned about their church's drift toward the secular would do well to consider. I will mention four.

Reaffirmation of faith. Underlying everything else in the evangelical, fundamentalist renewal happening in the United States is a reaffirmation of faith in the historical realities on which Christianity is grounded. I speak in particular about faith in the virgin birth, life, death, and resurrection of Jesus Christ.

I attended an Easter program recently at the First Church of the Nazarene in Nampa, Idaho—the town where Pacific Press is located. Nampa is dominated by the Nazarenes in much the same way that Takoma Park is dominated by the Adventists. Northwest Nazarene College is located in the town. The First Nazarene Church occupies most of two city blocks.

The Easter program was a live musical and dramatic pageant depicting the life, death, and resurrection of Christ, complete with live orchestra and choir, elaborate backdrops, and a cast of at least fifty people who had obviously learned and rehearsed their parts extremely well. "Jesus" rode a live donkey down the main aisle of the church, was "crucified" between two "thieves" at the front of the church, and actually "ascended," if not into heaven, at least into a layer of dark curtains up near the ceiling.

But the quality of the props and the skill of the actors was not what most impressed me. The life of Christ was juxtaposed with a conversation between several fervent Christians and a couple of Gentile skeptics. The play began with conversations between the skeptics and the Christians, and the dramatic portrayal of Christ's life was introduced as evidence that "convinced" the skeptics and eventually brought them to confess Him as Lord.

What inspired me more than I have been inspired in a long time was the ringing testimony of the Christians in the play—their expression of absolute faith in Jesus. Christ was a literal, historical Person who *really* died on the cross "for my sins" and who *really* rose from the tomb "for my salvation." The words "I believe" were repeated over and over, and always the belief was in Christ's life, death, and resurrection as real acts of God in human history.

Boldness. There is an unabashed boldness in the fundamentalist approach to secular society today. These people refuse to be intimidated by learning or by authority. No longer do they accept the secular-humanist control of education as inevitable and unavoidable. They have lost round after round in the courts over the teaching of creation in the public schools, but they get back up and try again. They learned from the civil rights activists of the sixties that he who stands up and speaks gets heard. Certain fundamentalists are determined to run their schools, day-care centers, and homes for wayward children free of government control of any sort, and they are not intimidated by laws or the police or the authority of the state.

This quality of boldness, of challenging secularism without apology or fear, was evident in the play I attended at the Nazarene Church in Nampa. One of the Romans in the play was a wealthy woman who came on stage beating her Christian slave and ridiculing the slave's religion. She assumed a haughty, scornful attitude toward all religion, and especially toward Christianity. The Christians simply affirmed their faith in Jesus and what He had done in their lives. At first the woman laughed, but the Christians maintained their confession of faith. This, together with the "view" of Christ's life played out in front of her, "converted" this scornful woman into a confessing, praying Christian.

The play was fictional, to be sure, in the sense that none of the actors were unbelievers and none of them were really converted that night. At the same time, the play was intensely real. It was obvious that the Christian actors were not just acting. *They really believed.*

There is still a lot of skepticism in liberal Christianity today. Liberal theologians are dissecting the Bible, questioning its historicity, and challenging its authority. Against this backdrop, the confession of the actors on the stage in the Nampa First Nazarene Church is a genuine statement of faith: "It doesn't matter what others think about Jesus. We know who we believe He was, and we know what His life means to us."

As I look at evangelical Christians around me in North America today, I am impressed that in spite of the hypocrisy we have seen in the lives of certain television evangelists, there is a resurgence of genuine old-time religion. In some ways it is a more intelligent faith than in times past, but it is still simple, bold, fearless faith.

The bold confession of the actors in the play was a reflection of this reality in contemporary evangelical Christianity.

Evangelism. Revitalized Protestant Christians in North America today have a worldwide evangelistic vision, and their actions match their words. The modern church growth movement is one of the best evidences of this. A consortium of evangelical agencies has set a goal of reaching the world by the year 2000, including plans to plant five million new churches all over the world in the next twelve years![1]

Again, the play I witnessed at the Nazarene Church in Nampa is an example of this revitalized evangelism in Protestant Christianity. At the close of the play, the church's pastor stood before a crowd of 2,000 people and made a call for commitment to Christ while the congregation sang "He Is Lord" several times.

There is a growing vision in evangelical Christianity of a world to be reached, and a sense that God has given us the responsibility of doing it, and therefore we will.

Planning. Finally, I would suggest that while the Holy Spirit is unquestionably moving on the hearts and minds of many of today's evangelicals and fundamentalists, they are not simply acting on inspiration. Entire institutions are being dedicated to the task, and well-laid plans are being developed for implementing the bold new vision. The new evangelical thrust is turning all the tools of modern scholarship to the study of how churches grow, and then teaching pastors and lay leaders how to do it.

This is not just the old frontier religion. It is the frontier religion's vision and faith in a very contemporary setting, deliberately using the methods and skills of our highly developed civilization to build up God's kingdom of grace, preparatory to the establishment of His kingdom of glory. This is a vision that grabs the attention of doctors, lawyers, engineers, wealthy Americans, influential Americans, and wins their commitment of time, talents, and money to the cause of Christ.

Other Characteristics of Adventist renewal

In addition to the points just mentioned, I will mention three others that I believe will characterize a renewed Adventism.

A worldwide work. First is a recapturing of our global vision. In 1874, thirty years after the disappointment, Adventists began spreading around the world. By the end of the century we were represented on every continent save Antarctica, and by 1950 we had work in nearly every country of the world.

No other Protestant denomination has achieved such a widespread work.

I do not say that proudly. To me, it is simply another indication that we *are* God's people. Whatever our failings of the past, we have to a large degree fulfilled the prediction of the first angel of Revelation 14 that God's final message on earth would go to "every nation, and kindred, and tongue, and people" (Revelation 14:6, KJV). God expects us to continue fulfilling that prophecy.

Youth Leadership. A second characteristic I look for in a renewed North American Adventism is leadership by young people. I do not have in mind so much administrative leadership of the denomination as I do evangelistic leadership at the local church level. In those parts of the world where Adventism is on fire and growing, young people are a significant part

of the church's forward thrust. Adventism beats in the hearts
of these young people. A fire for our message burns in their
souls. Adventist young people in these countries have a vision
for spreading the Adventist message. Young people are taking
the initiative. Young people are using their energies and their
creative imaginations to finish the work.

By contrast, North American Adventist youth are dropping
out of the church by droves. We are fortunate to keep 25 percent of our youth, and of these, very few understand that
Adventism's message is crucial to the world at the present
time.

A doctrine related to faith. Fortunately, there is a positive
way to view all of this, which brings me to the final characteristic that I look for in a renewed Adventism: a doctrine related to faith.

I am not wise enough to tell you why North American Adventist youth are dropping out of the church, but I will offer
one suggestion. Each generation of youth must redefine the vision of their forefathers in terms that have meaning for them.
Today's Adventist youth have not done that. Perhaps we have
not allowed them to. A majority of our youth see no significant
value for them or for the world in our message. That is why
they drop out.

But let's turn that around. There really *is* hope in all of
this. For all their seeming indifference, and in spite of the fact
that they are leaving the church by droves, I have utmost confidence that Adventist youth are still susceptible to the work
of the Holy Spirit. I believe that large numbers, even of those
who have abandoned this message for the time being, are still
latently committed to it and will return to it when, led by the
Spirit, they understand its true spiritual meaning for their
own lives.

I believe that three factors will be present when our young
people rediscover Adventism. First, they will study our message from both Scripture and the writings of Ellen White for
themselves, and they will reach conclusions faithful to what
these two inspired sources say. Second, they will challenge
those of us who are older in the church to return to the principle

of simplicity and self-sacrifice that got this church started, and which so many of us who are older have abandoned. And third, when today's Adventist youth capture the vision of our message in terms that make sense to them, they will be moved to do something about it. They will set in motion plans to share this message with others in their communities.

I have no doubt that in the very near future large numbers of younger Adventists will join with those of us who are older, and together, under the power of the latter rain, God will use all of us to reveal to the world, not merely the doctrinal teachings of our church, but the love of God that shines through those teachings. This will be the glorious "loud cry" that we have so long anticipated.

Yes, Adventism too

Adventism is in a state of change. But this change does not have to be toward the secular. We are not doomed to becoming more worldly. We *may* continue that way, but we don't *have* to. The resurgence of evangelical Christianity in North America today proves that it is possible to roll back the drift toward secularism, not only of individuals, but of whole institutions. It is entirely realistic to think that significant numbers of Adventist professional people—doctors, lawyers, engineers, and wealthy businessmen—will commit themselves to a renewed vision of the historical mission of our church. Some have already made that commitment. I believe that many more will in the very near future. And when that happens, it will set the world on fire.

Of one thing I am certain: A renewed Adventism in North America will be rooted in an unshakable faith—faith, first of all in the real Jesus who lived in *real* human history 2,000 years ago, and second, in the idea that God really *was* at work in the events surrounding the 1844 crisis that gave birth to our church.

Within a month after the disappointment, Ellen White received a vision in which she saw a light shining from beginning to end along the path, on which God's people were walking. An angel told her that this light was "the midnight cry"—

that is, the 1844 movement. The light shone along the path, that the saints' feet might not stumble. However, some "rashly denied the light behind them, and said it was not God that had led them out so far. The light behind them went out, leaving their feet in perfect darkness, and they stumbled and lost sight of the mark and of Jesus, and fell off the path down into the dark and wicked world below."[2]

The early disciples had faith, not only in Christ's death, which they saw, and in His resurrection, which they experienced as they fellowshiped with Him for forty days; they also had faith that He had gone to heaven to sit down at the right hand of the Father as their Mediator. They had faith that what He did on the cross was important, and what He was doing at that very moment in heaven was equally important.

I believe that we must place our faith in our own history— the 1844 movement on this earth—and also in the fact that Jesus did, indeed, begin a special work of ministry in the heavenly sanctuary that is of vital importance for men and women to understand. I do not believe there will ever be a revitalized Adventism apart from this faith in the reality of God's work in our history and His special work on behalf of the human race in the sanctuary today. I do not believe we will ever rise up and finish the work God has given us to do— there will never be a latter rain or a loud cry—apart from an unshakable faith in these things as truly historical and real. I do not believe individual Adventists today can expect to go through the end time without this understanding and this faith. If you are tempted to think that you can deny these realities and still be ready for the close of probation and the second coming of Christ, please read again the words of Ellen White:

Others rashly denied the light behind them and said it was not God that had led them out so far. The light behind them went out, leaving their feet in perfect darkness, and they stumbled and lost sight of the mark and of Jesus, and fell off the path down into the dark and wicked world below.[3]

I believe Adventists today stand on the threshold of stupendous events. Too many of us do not realize it because we live during the delay when life seems so ideal. However, each of us is even now sealing his or her eternal destiny. Either we believe the realities of our history and the mission God has for each of us as a part of His final movement in the world, or we are indifferent to that history and that mission. If we believe and act, we will be prepared, and we will go through to the end with Jesus. If we deny or ignore, we will be lost.

Each one must make this decision for himself. I don't think we have a lot of time to decide.

1. See *Christianity Today*, January 15, 1988, pp. 26-29.
2. *Testimonies for the Church*, vol. 1, p. 59.
3. *Early Writings*, p. 15.